Where the River Ran

The Story of the Peace

THELMA IRVINE

TouchWood
EDITIONS

Copyright © 2000 Thelma Irvine

Canadian Cataloguing in Publication Data

Irvine, Thelma, 1926-
    Where the river ran

    Includes bibliographical references and index.
    ISBN 0-920663-69-9

    1. Peace River Region (B.C. and Alta.)—History—Fiction. 2. Peace
River Region (B.C. and Alta.)—History—Poetry. I. Title.
PS8567.R853W53 2000   C813'.6   C00-910529-8
PR9199.3.I69W53 2000

First edition 2000

Horsdal & Schubart wishes to acknowledge Canada Council, Heritage
Canada through the Book Publishing Industry Development Program, and
of the British Columbia Arts Council for their fiscal support of our
publishing program.

Cover image by Sandra Irvine
Drawings by Leith Nance
Maps by Lana Fitzpatrick
Edited by Linda Field
Layout and design by Vancouver Desktop Publishing Centre

TOUCHWOOD EDITIONS
an imprint of Horsdal & Schubart Publishers Ltd.
Victoria/Surrey
touchwoodeditions@home.com

Printed in Canada

Dedicated to the mighty Peace
and
those who came there.

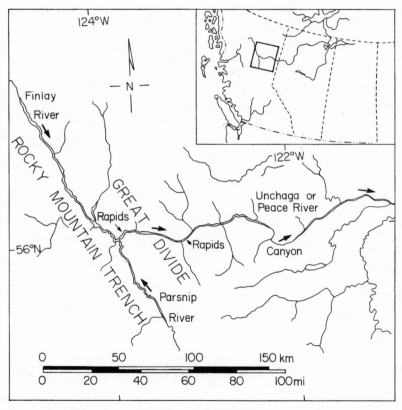

The Upper Regions of the Peace River (1780)

CONTENTS

ACKNOWLEDGEMENTS

Two books were invaluable in researching *Where the River Ran*. The first was *Peace River Chronicles*, edited by G.E. Bowes and published in 1963. This collection of writings by people who had travelled on the Peace provided ideas for many of the incidents in *Where the River Ran*. The book *Caesars of the Wilderness*, by Peter C. Newman, was the main source of information about the fur trade in the Athabasca region. Local histories from throughout the Peace district, and the dedicated people who prepared them, were also very much appreciated. Thanks go as well to friends and relatives for their suggestions and help.

The narrators in this book are fictitious. Many people and events are historical.

MAPS

FOREWORD

The Peace River, located in northern British Columbia and Alberta, is a major component of the Mackenzie River watershed. The upper part of this river, which is now a lake, was unique, as it passed through the Rocky Mountains from west to east. The river was changed in ancient times by glaciers, and in modern times by dams.

An undefined area surrounding the river is referred to as the Peace River country. This geographic entity, larger than the province of Nova Scotia, extends on both sides of the British Columbia/Alberta border to encompass mountains, foothills, and plains. The region has many resources, including the most northerly of Canada's agricultural lands. The Peace River country is isolated by the Rockies on the west and a dense corridor of non-arable forest to the south.

The location was one of the earliest known sites of human habitation in North America. Aboriginal people had been in the area for thousands of years before exploration by Europeans began in the late eighteenth century. The river played a significant role in the early fur trade in Canada, but, because of political events and physical remoteness, the region was one of the last to be settled by homesteaders.

The written history of the Peace includes exploration, fur trading, gold mining, the search for a railway pass, and the development of resources. *Where the River Ran* presents this history in a sequence of stories and poems.

This is the story of the Peace,
the river and the land.
It is a pageant of adventure
best told
by voices
from the past.

INVOCATION

Summon the forces that far in the past
Made seas into plains and mountains upcast
Planting the gold and the coal into seams
Melting the glaciers to running blue streams.

Summon the river that came from the west
To carve through the rock on its Arctic quest.
Summon the hunters of mammoth and moose
Who roamed through valleys the river cut loose.

Summon the spirits of those who were strong
Paddling upriver with vision and song
Drawing the maps and remembering to write
How the land in summer was north of night.

Summon the spirits of those who were bold
Who followed their dreams and sometimes found gold
Who travelled the trails to lead lonely lives
As northern lights danced in dark winter skies.

Summon the spirits of those who built homes
Who lived without roads or railways or phones
Summon them all from the mists of the dawn
Give them a voice in the river's long song.

THE RIVER

CHRONICLE

I am a Teller of Tales and I bring you the river's song.

The story begins in the eons of time before history, when oceans formed and continents moved apart. Look with me back in time, a hundred million years or more. The continent of North America is taking shape, but the place where the river will be is a shallow sea that comes and goes, over millions of years. A tropical swamp is created as the sea covers and uncovers the land. There are long-necked reptiles paddling like turtles in the water, while dinosaurs, with faces like ducks, roam in herds through evergreen forests. There are birds and fish and other types of dinosaurs as well. It is a world that none of you will ever know.

Move with me now to sixty million years ago. Everything has changed. The strange reptiles that paddled like turtles are gone. Only their skeletons remain. The dinosaurs with faces like ducks have vanished. Only their footprints can be seen. Instead of the forest and the sea there are grassy lakes and plains.

Look ahead, slowly, from that time. Mountains have started to form gradually, over thousands of years. The mountain ranges are creating walls for a thousand-mile-long trench where rivers will flow. A river is travelling down the trench from the north. It is cold and blue and has the strength of ice. It carries the glitter of gold. In the future it will be called the Finlay.

Another river is coming from the south. It is warmer and brown and brings the force of life. Someday it too will have a name. It will be called the Parsnip.

When these two rivers collide a new river will be born, one that will be known as the mighty Peace. This is the river I want to tell you about.

This river, born with the strength of ice and the force of life, was destined to flow in a new direction. It found a gap in the eastern wall of the trench and began travelling that way. Within a few miles there were obstacles. New mountains were forming, the ones that would be known as the Rockies. The mountains kept growing slowly, in the path of the river, but the river ruffled its waters into rapids as though to gather strength and cut through the rock of the mountains without changing course. It cut a passageway forty miles long and travelled swiftly on, while the mountains stood guard on either side.

When the river was beyond the mountains, it released its strength in more rapids, then rolled peacefully eastwards through the wide valley in the mountain foothills.

Now look again to the past. Focus on one million years ago. Once again, everything has changed. The mountains and the river are buried in ice. Glaciers are two miles thick. The ice, like the earlier sea, comes and goes over many more millennia.

Look now at fifteen thousand years ago. The land is warming and the glaciers are melting. The river is coming to life, but is blocked by a glacier at a rocky ridge of foothills forty miles east of the mountains. All the earth and rock that the glacier collected through the years is in the old path of the river.

Let me tell you what happens. The river was destined to travel eastward, even though its path was blocked. It turned sharply to the right and found a narrow gate in the rocks, one that a man could throw a stone across. All the water from the broad valley of the foothills crashed and thundered through the gate and created a canyon in the shape of a giant horseshoe. The water dropped over two hundred feet as it tumbled the twenty-mile distance. The force of the water smoothed the jagged canyon walls and created strange holes and fissures. The canyon was three hundred feet deep in most places, and the sound of the furious water broke the silence of the wilderness as it echoed into the land above.

Once through the canyon the river was able to spread out across the waiting plains. Patiently and gently, over the years, it carved a deep valley that reached eastward for two hundred and forty miles.

Finally, the river was tranquil. It turned north through lower lands and mingled with other rivers that journeyed to the ocean of the north, the Arctic.

That is how the river and the land around it came to be.

Listen now as I tell you of the people who came to the river. Look to the past again with me. It is ten thousand years ago. The valleys of the river hold new life. There are woolly mammoths with tusks, bison with big horns, and all kinds of other animals, some big and some small. Human families are travelling the trench and the river valleys, hunting for food.

In a few thousand years the mammoths have vanished and only their skeletons remain near the canyon. The climate changes from warmer to colder, then to warmer again.

The animals move with the changes to where they can find food. The people move with the animals. Some go eastward, like the river, and spread across the continent. Some stay with the river. They hunt with spears and cook their food over fires.

In other parts of the world, great pyramids are being built, and empires are being won and lost. The river, though, remains unchanged. It flows swiftly through the mountains, the foothills, and the plains, and except at the rapids on each side of the mountains, and in the canyon where only water can move, it appears smooth and constant. It is known only by the people who walk nearby.

Listen.

A DREAMER SPEAKS[1]

I speak for the Dunne-za
the real people
whom you know as the people of the Beaver.

We have known the river
forever
moving like the water
over rocks and hills and plains
hunting
always hunting.

When great beasts consumed us
the hunter Saya destroyed them
and brought new animals to us
and taught us their ways.
We were all part of the same world
and our children were wise.

The dreams of our hunters
showed us the trails
in the woods along the river.
We walked together in the cold
and hunted with the bow and the snare.
The bison and bear, the moose and the elk
all came to us
when we needed them

---

1   See note on page 154.

and let us close around them
for the kill.
If we were hungry
it was because we did not remember
their ways.

In the long days of the sun
we followed the trails
to the gathering place by the river
to share our songs.
When the drums
brought songs of battles
with those from beyond the river,
whose talk was as strange
as the sound of the jay,
we were frightened.
These enemies took the skins of the beavers
to others with faces of white
who gave them weapons to carry
that killed with shooting fire.

Our hunters listened to the sad songs of death
and dreamed of new trails
near the place
where the sun sets
on the river.
We left the level lands
and hunted in the great valleys and hills.
The people who were there
moved to the land beyond the canyon
that we did not know.
We fought in all directions
and the golden leaves trembled
at the sound

for we, too, found the weapons of fire.
Our enemies to the east
whom you call the Cree
became weak with a strange sickness
that moved our way.
We had victory in battle
and it was time for peace.
We met
on the river
and smoked the pipe
on the point we called
Unchagah,
Point of Peace.
Our River of Beavers
became
the River of Peace
and peace flowed on with the river,
but the world
beyond the river
brought us change.

FORTS AND FURS

CHRONICLE

Take a look with me at the world far beyond the river. Men from
Europe have learned to sail the seas and have reached North
America. Boatloads of people have crossed the stormy Atlantic to
start new lives. They have built homes and cities along the eastern
coast and, like a thin wall of people walking across the land, their
settlements are gradually moving westwards.

Look at the west coast. Ships are sailing in those seas as well.
The captains are drawing maps of the coastline and meeting the
native people who live there. In the central part of the continent,
there are many miles where the buffalo still thunder across the
plains, undisturbed as yet by the advancing settlements.

The northern half of the continent, where there is often so much
snow and ice, has changed very little. French families live near the
native families along the shores of the St. Lawrence River, and
English people are on the shores of the eastern Great Lakes. Some
men from those settlements have learned from the native people
how to travel in canoes and have followed the rivers west. A few
have paddled far enough to see the Rocky Mountains on the
horizon and wonder if men and canoes will ever go beyond.

On the shores of the Hudson Bay, there are a few forts where
traders of the Hudson's Bay Company wait for native people to
bring them furs. There are other forts along the rivers of the west
where traders of the North West Company meet other natives who
bring them furs. The native people leave the forts with knives and
axes, pots and blankets, traps and guns, and return in a few
months with more furs, mostly beaver, while the traders from both
companies compete to see which company can ship the most furs
to Europe.

Near the place where the waters of the Unchaga mingle with the rivers that flow to the Arctic, there is a large lake. On the shores of this lake, high up on a hill, is a group of log buildings called Fort Chipewyan. It is a North West Company fort and it is the only fort for hundreds of miles. Men arrive there by canoe, shouting and singing, men with strong arms who have paddled and portaged for seventy-five days. They are voyageurs, called Men of the North. They bring the trade goods that will be exchanged for furs. They know they are in a land that is rich with beaver and marten.

The men inside the fort make plans as they wait for the voyageurs. They are certain that if they explore all the rivers, they will find one that will take them west beyond the Rocky Mountains. One man, Alexander Mackenzie, plans to build a small fort on the shores of the Unchaga. He will build it at the most westerly position he knows of, near the point where the Dunne-za and the Cree made peace. He will spend the winter there, and in the spring, he will follow the river west. When he reaches the canyon, he will be as determined to cross the Rockies as the river was, so long ago, when it carved its way in the opposite direction.

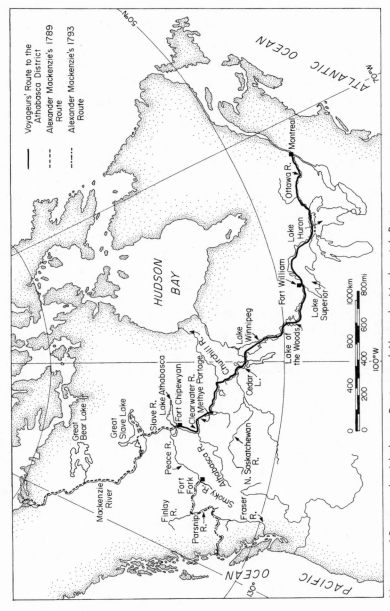

Voyageurs' Route to the Athabasca Region and Alexander Mackenzie's Routes
Travel time: Montreal to Fort William, about 50 days / Fort William to Fort Chipewyan, about 75 days.

Legend:
Voyageurs' Route to the Athabasca District
Alexander Mackenzie's 1789 Route
Alexander Mackenzie's 1793 Route

THE CANYON

1793

"The man is crazy," said Jacques. "We'll never get through here." His hands were still numb from holding the tracking line.

"Aye, but he's brave," said MacKay, his words almost lost in the noise of the rapids as the river, cold and furious, sprayed the rocks below their fire.

"I'm as brave as any man," said Jacques, "but we'll not make this. This is a devil's canyon. The Indians don't go here. They use a trail, a carrying trail. We should go back to the Fort."

The other voyageurs nodded. They had spent two days dragging and pulling a canoe through rapid after rapid, some stumbling over rocks on shore with the lines, the others soaked and shivering in the boat.

"Four portages in two miles," continued Jacques, "and then the bow-line breaking like that, in that fast water. You could all have been smashed to pieces."

"Providence pushed us to shore," said François. "That's how we cleared the rocks, and then you were there, Jacques, to hold the canoe. And the canoe, not even damaged. It was a miracle."

It was a miracle, thought MacKay, and this is a devil's canyon. He had never seen one like it. No wonder they were frightened.

He left the six men drinking their rum at the fire and went to join their leader.

Alexander Mackenzie stood at the edge of the river, looking upstream. As far as he could see in the afternoon light, the river, enclosed by rock cliffs, was a sheet of white, foaming water. It hardly seemed the same Unchaga, River of Peace, that they had travelled the first ten days out of the Fort. Then, even with the stiff current, they had made fifteen hours of progress a day. There had always been gravel bars for landing, and trees and game on the high sloping banks. He had described it in his journal as a most magnificent theatre of nature, one of the finest he had seen in this God-forsaken land. But now the strength of this broad river was confined in a fifty-yard chasm and there were no more fresh leaves or blossoms to remind him of spring.

Mackenzie turned as his second-in-command approached. "It has been a hard day Mr. MacKay."

"The men are restless, sir. They want to turn back."

"I never turn back," said Mackenzie, "and neither will they. Have them make camp further up the bank and tell them there will be extra rest in the morning."

He beckoned to the two native guides who stood by the canoe. "We'll make our way up the canyon and see what's ahead."

MacKay watched them go, twenty-nine-year-old Mackenzie in the lead, still energetic after the difficult day. They soon disappeared around the bend in the river, moving more like animals than men, hands and feet gripping the sharp, wet rocks.

MacKay returned to the fire to give his instructions. "We'll make camp higher up while they scout ahead," he told the voyageurs.

"Some dry ground, away from the river, that would be better," said Jacques.

"And the work will warm us," said François.

They worked together, MacKay leading, the other six men swinging axes with the same unified rhythm they used when paddling. As the long daylight hours of the northern spring evening continued, brush was cleared, steps were chipped, and an angled, upward trail took shape. By dusk they had reached a flat area suitable for an encampment and had carried up the goods needed for the night. Fire and food were waiting when Mackenzie and his guides arrived back, their footwear and clothing torn.

"We are exhausted," said Mackenzie as they joined the men by the fire. "It was good to find your fine trail."

"And how does it look, the river ahead?" asked Jacques.

"We cannot proceed by water," said Mackenzie, removing his boots. "We saw no end to the rapids."

"Those Indians, where we spent the night before this canyon, they told us we could not pass through here. They said there was a trail." Jacques stood up as he spoke.

"We have missed the trail, I'm sure," said François. "Sit down, Jacques, and listen."

"That trail is no safer than the river, Jacques," said MacKay. "The enemies of those people wait there in ambush."

"My God, what a country." Jacques sat down again, cross-legged and hunched by the fire.

"The river does not exist that you voyageurs cannot conquer," said Mackenzie. "We will make plans in the morning."

Gradually, as the woods darkened around them, the men quietened and slept. Only Mackenzie remained awake, watching the sparks from the burning spruce log splatter, like new stars, before him. The flames made shapes and shadows that taunted him.

He must reach the Pacific. He must not be wrong again. Reaching that frozen northern sea two years ago, many had said it was a great accomplishment, but his disappointment had been agony. All his time since had been spent studying and planning. There had been one long winter in England, learning navigation and astronomy, and then another winter, as far west as possible, at Fort Fork. What a winter it had been, cold and dark, trading furs and making preparations. He had talked to every native person he saw, to learn about the country, and had chosen the best of men to travel with him. Then, after the canoe had been packed and ready, there had been the waiting, waiting for the ice to leave the river. So much time. So many plans. He must succeed.

He looked at the sky. The stars told him that he was travelling west. This had to be the river, the one that would take him through these silent mountains and show him a northwest passage. He and his men would make a long portage. They would move their canoe and baggage, three thousand heavy pounds, up from the river and cut a trail through the woods, maybe for ten or twelve miles, until the river was navigable again. He would leave the awful force of water in this huge canyon for men of the future to conquer. His task was to reach the Pacific. The stars were constant in the sky. His men were the best of voyageurs. He was an able leader. They would succeed.

And soon he, too, slept.

CHRONICLE²

Alexander Mackenzie did succeed. Ninety-six days later he and his men were back at the Fort, near the Point of Peace, having reached the Pacific and returned. The following year he returned to the east and told others how he had followed the Unchaga through the Rockies.

He told them of the canyon, so dangerous that it couldn't be navigated; of the terrible portage over swamps and hills and fallen trees; of the rapids on either side of the mountains; and of the steep precipices topped with snow that pressed in on the river as the water moved with the wind through the pass. He told them of the two rivers that gave birth to the Peace, one to the north that vanished into more mountains, and the other to the south that led to the three small lakes along the portage to the western watershed. He told them of the abundance of beaver and marten and bear, of buffalo and elk, and of coal in the walls of the canyon. He told them of the people living in that land, the Sekani, the Beaver, and the Cree.

Other men listened and within a few years they too travelled to the river. John Finlay paddled the parent streams. David Thompson walked the banks and drew maps. Simon Fraser brought men to build forts for the North West Company. They started below the canyon, building Rocky Mountain Portage House on the south bank of the river. Fraser and some of his men endured the portage, lined their canoes through the first set of rapids, and portaged around the second set to travel west and south. They built a chain of forts beyond the Rockies on rivers that

---

2 See note on page 155.

led to the Pacific; Fort Macleod, Fort St. James, Fort Fraser, Fort George. They returned to the Peace. About sixty miles below the canyon they built Fort St. John and beyond that, Fort Dunvegan. From there the canoes could travel to Fort Vermilion and Fort Chipewyan and on to the waterways and portages that led across the continent to the settlement of Montreal. The North West Company was in firm control of the fur trade along the Peace, but once again, events beyond the river were to bring change.

The rivalry between the Hudson's Bay Company and the North West Company had become intense and bitter. The conflict came to the shores of the Peace as the Hudson's Bay Company built rival forts in the area. The fighting threatened to destroy both companies. It ended only when the two companies joined together under the Hudson's Bay Company name.

In 1821, all the forts on the Peace, including Rocky Mountain Portage House, Fort St. John, Fort Dunvegan, and Fort Vermilion, became Hudson's Bay Company forts, and the Unchaga was once again the River of Peace.

Listen to the voices from that time.

A DREAMER SPEAKS

1820

We called from the banks of the river
as the white men came in their strong canoes.
We camped near their forts
and learned their names.
Our hunter
flew
in his dream
like a swan
to the land of another season,
to the spirit land beyond the sky
where all that can be learned is known.
He saw
that the trails we had walked together
would no longer show us the way.
We would forget the path of the moose and the deer
and live among the people who came
to learn new ways.
Already we knew the force of our guns
and our River of Beavers had a new name.
We heard his words
and set our traps
for furs.

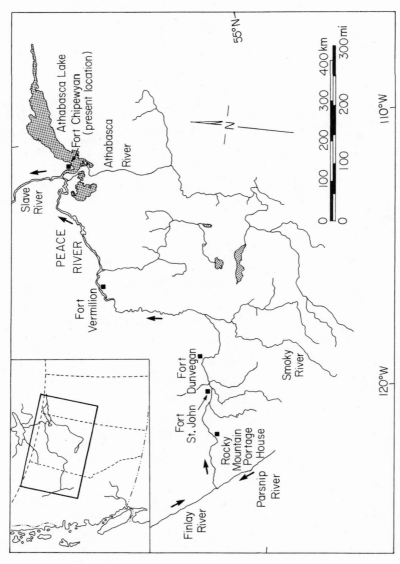

Major Forts on the Peace (1823)

A MONOLOGUE AT THE PEACE

1821

It's about time all this fighting stopped. It used to be that getting furs was the important thing, that and staying alive in the winter. The last few years have been one long battle to see which company was going to win. I've always been a North West Company man myself and I like it that way. There's lots of work to do at this post, and with all the silence around, there's lots of time to think. Sometimes, if it's been quiet for too long, I talk to myself about what is going on in other places. The men who stop by, coming and going to Fort Chipewyan, tell me all about things.

I guess the fighting had to happen. When Turnor came up here about thirty years ago he tried to claim all this country for the Bay; said that the rivers drained east and the Athabasca region was part of Rupert's Land. Of course he was wrong. You only have to cross the Methye Portage once to know that. You can easily see the river valley running north from there. All these rivers drain north. That's why the Nor'Westers up here are so proud. They get baptized with northern water in a special ceremony the first time they go over that portage, and they swear allegiance to the Northman's code. It makes them feel special. It saves a lot of trouble too, because they have to promise not to kiss another Northman's wife without permission.

33

Well, Turnor sent Fidler up here anyway, about 1802, to build a fort for the Bay. He built it not too far from Fort Chipewyan and called it Nottingham House. Don't know why he chose such a fancy name for a simple log building. Fort Chipewyan was a much grander place. When Fidler started to trade he had a hard time. That man of ours, Samuel Black, made his life a misery. He stole his fish. He burned his wood. He even killed his dog and ate it! One day he climbed up on the roof of the Bay fort and blocked the chimney. The men in there came out sputtering pretty quick, almost dead. There were a lot of good men in the North West Company, but that man Black was an ugly one. He could howl like a wolf at night and send shivers up any man's spine.

Fidler left in a few years and then things went on as usual. The Bay built a few little posts along the Peace, but not much changed 'til that trouble at Seven Oaks. One of the fellows who escaped after that massacre told me all about it. He'd come here hoping to miss any more trouble. He said that Semple's men dropped like rabbits, shot one by one. And no wonder! There were only a few of them, a couple of dozen, riding out. Mr. Semple thought he was so important that he could just talk to Cuthbert Grant and make him and his big crowd of men leave without a shot being fired. But every man in that crowd was angry. Semple had burned their fort, and the settlers at Red River were keeping the pemmican from reaching our men in the canoes. You can't keep food away from men and expect peace! The canoes had to get to Fort Chipewyan and back every year before the ice came. Those men needed that pemmican. Grant's men started shooting and kept it up until not one of Semple's men was left.

It's a funny thing, but that poor Metis man who told me all this did end his troubles by coming up here. He drowned in the river the next spring. I don't think he ever forgot about those hacked-up bodies that were left lying on the ground.

I guess things were pretty bad back east after that. Selkirk took over Fort William for the Bay and then recaptured Fort Douglas.

There wasn't much to stop a Bay man like John Clarke from coming north. He was another nasty man. He liked to flick gunpowder in men's eyes. They say he used to hit men with his cane and that his cane was decorated with diamonds. He built another fort for the Bay, about a mile and a half from Fort Chipewyan. Called it Fort Wedderburn. Then he set out up the Peace to reclaim all the little forts that the Bay had lost. I wrote a song about that trip of his. I like to have something to sing when I'm alone. It goes like this:

Fifty strong men paddled up the Peace
Fifty strong men from the Bay
Fifty strong men without any food
Needing to hunt on the way.

Nor'Wester men crept on the banks
Nor'Westers sent out by Black
Nor'Westers chased all the game away
Forcing the Bay men back.

Thirty Bay men came down the Peace
Leaving their dead behind
Nor'Westers hid bags of pemmican
For starving men to find.

Hungry men from the Hudson's Bay
Stumbled into the Fort
"You're charged with theft of pemmican"
Said Mr. Black, holding court.

The men of the Bay paddled back east
And promised to stay away
And so the men of the great North West
Conquered the men of the Bay.

That was the end of the Bay around here for a while, until Robertson came. He brought two hundred armed men with him and tried to live like a king. He had special wine and fancy food and he gave liquor to the Indians. He wasn't the first man to do that. Nor'Westers had done it for years. They say some Nor'Westers were killed a few years ago, when Indians saw what liquor was doing to their people.

Well, Robertson was outside one day, conducting a funeral, and Mr. Black walked up and captured him. Black kept him prisoner for quite a while before he sent him back east. I guess Robertson escaped somewhere along the way.

It wasn't until Mr. Simpson arrived that things settled down. Mr. Simpson was smart. He cut expenses and bribed the Indians. He even managed to trick that young McGillivray at Fort Chipewyan and take him prisoner. That was a funny thing. Simpson decided that McGillivray could have his wife stay with him at the prison. One night McGillivray escaped wearing his wife's nightgown and ran back to his own fort. The Nor'Westers did lots of hooting and hollering about that!

Before Mr. Simpson left, he was making lots of money for the Bay. In fact, the Bay was starting to be more like the North West Company used to be in the old days, very successful.

Now I've been told that the fight is over. The two companies are going to join together under the Hudson's Bay Company name. It's kind of sad to think that there will no longer be men called Nor'Westers. This part of the country won't be the same without them. I'll be a Hudson's Bay Company man now myself, whether I like it or not. At least the name of the river hasn't changed. It will still be called the Peace River and the name will start making some sense again.

THE VOICE OF THE VOYAGEUR

1823

I sing for the men of the river
Who worked for the Hudson's Bay
They wanted only to paddle
And be on the water each day.

But a tale of death and betrayal
Is heard in this sad song.
Who knows the truth of the story?
Who knows the right or the wrong?

The fort on the banks of the river
Was called the Fort of St. John.
There were meadows near the buildings
That Indians camped upon.

The trading was done in the store
The man in command was Hughes.
The goods and furs were moved
In voyageur-like canoes.

As Peace was the name of the river
So peace remained at the Fort
'Til a canoe arrived from Dunvegan
With a man of a different sort.

Bad men of all breeds
Bring with them bad deeds
And Black was just such a man.
As Black was his name,
Dark too was his fame
Mr. Black, whose first name was Sam.

Some hated the man
And knew of his plan
To steal an Indian's wife.
And all were in fear
For they knew in his gear
He carried both pistol and knife.

The peace at the Fort was uncertain
When Black finally left with his crew
Then orders arrived from Dunvegan.
The Fort was to move somewhere new.

Upriver to Mountain Portage House
Went load after load in canoes.
Hughes walked alone near the river
To give his neighbours the news.

The Indians camped in the meadow,
Heard what Mr. Hughes said.
It only deepened their sadness
For one of their own was dead.

Angry ones planned an ambush.
They vowed they had been betrayed
For a fort at Mountain Portage House
Would with their enemies trade.

Bad men of all breeds
Bring with them bad deeds
And always there are such ones.

Guy Hughes was shot by the river
Guy Hughes was dragged to the store
Guy Hughes was left there dying
He'd not buy furs any more.

Sing for the men of the river
Who worked for the Hudson's Bay
Who sang to the dip of their paddles
And returned to the Fort next day.

A call came over the water
From an Indian woman on shore.
"Go back, go back, I beg you.
It's not safe for you here anymore."

But shots flew over the water.
The paddlers' songs were stilled.
And bodies fell into the river
As four good men were killed.

The woman called out in the silence
As another canoe came by.
"There's danger, danger, danger.
If you land you will surely die."

The men on the river heard her
And left with faces pale.
They raced to Fort Dunvegan
To tell the grisly tale.

The wind on the shore blew softly.
The Indians crept away
And only the dogs that were barking
Were alive at the Fort that day.

Who knows the end of this story?
Who knows the right and the wrong?
Only the ghosts on the river know
In the mists near Fort St. John.

THE CANYON

1828

My name is Bear, Bear Boucher. I've been travelling up and down this river for over twenty years. I've seen a lot of strange things in that time, but nothing has been as amazing as what I've seen on this trip.

It's because I know the river so well that Governor Simpson asked me to travel with him. The agent at Dunvegan told him that I'd been over the portage a few times and that I knew the route to Macleod's Lake. He said, too, that I'd know the best places to stop along the way, like this place where we are camped right now. There's a little stream here that flows into the Unchaga and there's a good level gravel bar with lots of driftwood. It's a pretty spot too, with the narrow valley and all the colours of fall starting to show; something I thought the Governor's wife would enjoy.

The last time I travelled above the canyon like this I was with Mr. Black. He was on his way up the Finlay. I've been at most of the places below the canyon too. I've worked at the Portage House and at Fort St. John and even back at Fort Chipewyan. The Hudson's Bay was happy to keep me on after the merger because I'm pretty good at languages. I lived with the priests back east while I was growing up.

I've been at Fort Dunvegan for a few years now. In fact, I was there when the news came about the massacre. All the forts on the Peace were closed after that sad day, so I went to Vermilion and trapped. When Dunvegan opened again I was hired back. It's been busy. There's a lot of damage done to an empty fort in three years time.

Canoes don't usually go up river from Dunvegan anymore. Fort St. John and Rocky Mountain Portage House are still closed, so there are no white men living between Dunvegan and Macleod Lake. There are only Indians, and I hear they are starving.

It was quite a sight when the Governor's party arrived at Dunvegan that day. I was chopping wood outside the fort when I heard a sound as strange as was ever heard in those forests. It was the sound of a bugle. I thought for a moment that Gabriel himself had come for me, but when I looked up I saw a loaded canoe in the distance. It was carrying at least a dozen men. Then a second canoe came in sight and I heard the sound of a cannon. It was as though thunder came from the river, not the sky. The agent was outside with me by that time. I saw tears come to his eyes as bagpipe music started drifting towards us. I'm sure he wished he was back in the land of the Scots that he had left so long ago. Then came a sound I had longed to hear, the sound of men's voices singing the old songs of the voyageurs. They were as sweet to me as the songs of angels, and I was a happy man as I watched the sunlight flashing off the paddles in time to the music.

The second canoe was as loaded as the first. When it came closer, a man in the centre stood up. He was wearing a fine red tartan cloak and a tall beaver hat. He looked as grand as any king. When I saw the Union Jack waving away on the stern of the canoe, I knew that it could only be the Governor-in-Chief of the Hudson's Bay Company who was arriving. I could hardly believe it when I saw a woman as well, in the same canoe. She was carried ashore on the back of one of the men.

The Governor, Mr. Simpson, did not know me, but I remembered him. I had seen him before, at the very same place, Fort

Dunvegan, almost six years earlier. Mr. Simpson had arrived in the middle of winter. He had been all the way up to Great Slave Lake and back to Fort Chipewyan on snowshoes and had come up the Peace the same way. Even the Indians were impressed. Some of them travelled on with him across the snow to Lesser Slave Lake and Fort Edmonton. I'd heard that, since then, Mr. Simpson crossed the mountains farther south, though why any man would want to ride a horse or walk when they could travel by canoe, I'll never understand. Knowing all this about Mr. Simpson, I wasn't surprised to learn that he was headed to the Pacific.

The party rested for a day at the Fort. They had come all the way from York Factory on Hudson Bay in just over six weeks. A lot of the canoe men were Iroquois so I couldn't understand everything they said. I did figure out that the lead man, the head guide, was called Bernard. He was a big man with a strong face and was full of energy and fun. He signalled to the Indians camped at the Fort that Mr. Simpson's dog could talk. Then he tied a music box around the dog's neck and made it play. Pouce Coupe and the others were most entertained. I could understand what they were saying, of course. They were making comments about the way the piper was dressed and how his music sounded like a sick goose. It was a merry day in all, and a happy change in routine.

In the dark early the next morning, someone shouted, "Levez, levez." Mr. Simpson had given orders that we were to leave at daybreak. The send-off was quiet because there weren't many people at the fort. They did their best to give us a cheer as Mr. Simpson had ordered.

The current above Dunvegan is strong, but the canoes made good time. Each canoe had nine men with paddles, and they never missed a stroke. I could see Mr. Simpson ahead in the lead canoe. He sometimes looked like he was sleeping, but then his hand would dangle over the side. He'd be checking the speed of the canoe by trailing his fingers in the water. If he didn't think it was fast enough he'd call out to Bernard, the Iroquois guide. Bernard wouldn't answer. He'd just look ahead and speed up the rate of his strokes. Only the strong could survive with Mr. Simpson.

We camped each night on the river banks. The river is low in September, so it was not too difficult for the Iroquois to carry the travellers to shore. There was the Chief Factor, Archibald MacDonald, and the Doctor, Richard Hamlyn, and, of course, Mr. Simpson and his wife Margaret. I guess she was really a country wife, for she was the sister of the servant, Tom Taylor, and he was of mixed blood. The piper and myself, of course, would not let any man carry us.

In the evenings Mr. Simpson and Mr. MacDonald would write in their journals. I heard them talking about the beauty and grandeur of the scenery and the rich soil.

We didn't stop where the old Fort St. John had been because the buildings had been burned. On the fifth morning, I showed them where the portage began, on the shore opposite the old Rocky Mountain Portage House.

I knew that getting over the portage would be harder than getting into heaven, as no one had travelled that way for over three years. When I told Mr. Simpson that, he decided the canoes should not be portaged. He announced that Bernard and the seven other Iroquois men were to take the empty canoes through the canyon while the rest of us carried the goods over the portage.

"Mr. Simpson," I said, "a trip through the canyon is impossible. It is twenty miles long. The canoes will be destroyed and the men will drown."

Mr. Simpson pretended not to hear. Bernard heard me, though, and he knew what I was saying.

Mr. Simpson started talking to Bernard. I could understand enough to know what he was talking about. He was saying that Bernard and his men could go up any cascade, that if they couldn't paddle they would walk, that if they couldn't walk they would probably fly, that they were as much at ease on the river as the ducks that we could see swimming near the shore were.

Bernard stood up very straight. His face didn't change at all. He called to his men and they started preparing lines for the empty canoes. I told him, with signs and words, how he would recognize the upper end of the portage. In my heart I shuddered to think what was ahead and doubted that I would see any of them again. I had once looked over the canyon wall at the upper end and had seen logs turn into splinters as they crashed from one wall of rock to the other. I had talked to Indians who had seen parts of the canyon in winter when the water was frozen. They said that in most places there was no escape because the topmost ledge of rock hung out over the water, it was so hollowed out below from the force of the river. I knew there would be fierce rapids and whirlpools and waterfalls, with nothing on the canyon walls to hold onto. The only trees that could grow in such a place would be those that clung to crevices high above the river.

I watched Bernard and the men leave, four men paddling in each canoe. They were out of sight in no time.

Mr. Simpson turned to the rest of us and said that whoever made it over the portage with his share of cargo would be able to call himself a man. I saw his wife smile at her brother about this. She was a strong lady, though, and she always kept up with us.

There was a lot of swearing, even though a lady was present, as we hacked our way over the trail. The first mile took us four hours. At the end of the second day I went ahead with Mr. Simpson and some others to clear the trail a bit. We came back in the morning and helped the others with the cargo. All the while I was thinking about the men with the canoes, hoping that at least an eagle high above the canyon would witness them pulling and poling the canoes and maybe slipping over the rocks to their deaths.

By midday, we were along the trail about another four miles. We all stopped suddenly when we heard voices. When you hear voices in the wilderness like that, you wonder if you are going mad, or if maybe you are being ambushed. Mr. Simpson gave a loud "Hello," and who answered but Bernard! There he was, coming to meet us, with all his crew. We greeted them like heroes. They had survived the canyon and returned on the portage to help with the load. Apparently Bernard and the other men in his canoe had almost gone to perdition. The canoe had filled with water while they were lining it up a rapid. It had been so heavy and the current so strong that Bernard was pulled from the rocks into the torrent. He had somehow reached the canoe and turned it over, and the others were able to pull him back to the ledge. His hands were scraped and his clothing was in shreds.

We were only three miles from the river when we camped that night, so we reached the canoes the next morning. The rest of that day we repaired the canoes and rested. We came safely through the first rapids, and today we pulled into this spot. It was when we got on shore here that I decided to write this story. It should be more than eagles who know that men went through that canyon and survived. Bernard made it known to me tonight that it was a miracle they had made it through, that such a journey would be impossible if the water had been any higher.

Just a few more words about today. We made good time. When we pulled in to shore, Bernard carefully carried Margaret from the canoe and went back for Mr. Simpson. He had him securely on his back and was standing in water about two feet deep. He looked around at those of us on shore, grinned, and fell. Mr. Simpson was in the water, boots, coat, hat, and all, sputtering and splashing. Bernard stood up and offered him a hand. "Mr. Simpson," he said, in words we could all understand, "you are as clever as a duck in the water."

Margaret laughed the most. Mr. Simpson's servant soon had him warm and dry. In the evening, when Mr. MacDonald was writing in his journal, he asked me the name of the creek that was beside us. I thought for a moment and said, "The creek is named Bernard." There were cheers from everyone, even Mr. Simpson.

JOURNEYS

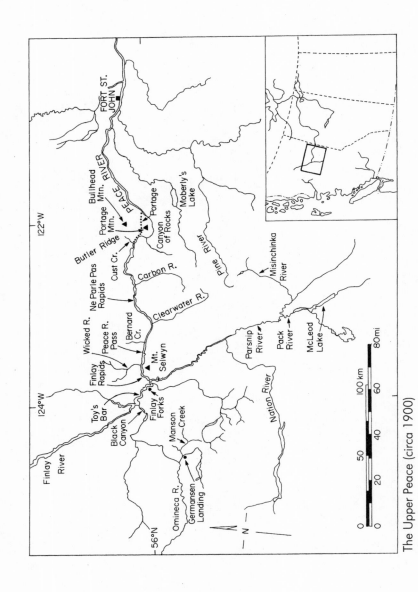

The Upper Peace (circa 1900)

48

CHRONICLE

Governor Simpson reached the Pacific. His Iroquois crew navigated even the formidable Fraser Canyon. That part of the trip was so terrible that the plan for a trade route to the Pacific using the Peace and Fraser rivers was abandoned. Trading went south from Dunvegan to Fort Edmonton and travel across the Rockies went overland to the Columbia River.

For over thirty years the land of the Peace was unchanged. The region was as isolated as an island. Voyageurs vanished from the river and only native bands roamed the ancient trails.

There were many changes beyond the river. American settlements moved farther west and the country of Canada took shape. Upper and Lower Canada were united and the colony of British Columbia was established. The steam locomotive was invented in England and railways were built in the eastern regions of North America. Gold was discovered, first in California, then in the Cariboo. People, hoping to find fortunes, rushed to these places.

In 1861 a gold strike was reported near the mouth of the Parsnip River. Men went north. The first few were followed by hundreds. Some found gold and survived. The majority left, disillusioned.

The successful miners were a special breed. They were a new kind of nomad who shared the northern edge of civilization with the aboriginal people. They trapped in winter and mined in summer and felt that the whole wild, wonderful country belonged to them.

NOMADS ON THE PEACE

1862 – 1875

My name is Peace River Smith. I want to tell you about a man I knew who was so big, so strong, and so rich that you'll hardly believe he was real. His name was Pete Toy.

I first met Pete in 1862 at Fort St. John. I was a young man then. The fort had only been reopened for a couple of years and my partner and I were there doing a little work to earn some provisions before we moved on. My partner was Black Jack Jones. He had quite a reputation as a card player. Mr. Kennedy at the Fort gave me the name of Peace River to go with Smith because I fell in the river the first time I tried to unload one of those round-bottomed canoes. I didn't mind having a change of name because my reputation with my old name hadn't been too good down on the Fraser. Those were the days when people were looking for gold all up and down the mountains of North America, hoping to strike it rich. Being greedy for gold can make men do strange things.

Pete and his partner Joe pulled their canoe up on shore at Fort St. John late one afternoon. I noticed Pete right away. He had the broad shoulders of someone who had swung an axe a lot, and he seemed to stretch way above the rest of us. His hair was black and curly, and you could hardly tell what was hair and what was beard. His feet were big and his boots looked heavy as he stepped out of that canoe. He'd been on the river for days, but he was still tidy, with his shirt tucked in and no holes in his trousers. I think it was his blue shirt that made his eyes look so blue. When he laughed he would throw back his head and his eyes would disappear into the creases on his face. That's the picture of him that I always have in my mind; a big, strong, happy man stepping onto the shore from a canoe.

The days were so long right then that we had a good chance to talk after supper. We talked about the gold strike on the Parsnip that Bill Cust and Ed Carey had made.

"There are a lot of men coming north now," said Pete.

"They are even moving the boundary of the colony," said Mr. Kennedy. "I had a letter about it. British Columbia wants to be sure it owns all the rivers that might have gold."

The politics about boundaries didn't interest me much, but a chance to travel along to the gold strike with someone like Pete Toy seemed like a piece of good luck. I asked Pete if Black Jack and I could join them. He and Joe agreed, and they even helped us next day to finish the dugout canoe we'd been working on.

We weren't out on the river long before I knew we'd made a good choice. Pete Toy could catch fish or spot game faster than anyone I'd known. It seemed like he'd have a fire going and bannock and tea made almost as soon as we'd make camp. He carried far more than his share through the portage, and I think he took note of every tree and rock along the way, he was so at home in the wilderness. On the river he could paddle or pole with a strength that was more than the other three of us put together. I doubt if we would have made it through the first rapids without him.

Mr. Kennedy had told us to pole through on the north shore. The water was so smooth that it looked safe from a distance, but really it was dropping terribly fast without any warning sounds over wide reefs. Guess that's why those rapids are called the Ne Parle Pas Rapids now. We could have been swamped, going upstream like that, before we knew we were in danger. Pete, though, seemed to have a sixth sense about rivers. He had us out on shore while the current was still steady. We took the canoes through one at a time, two men in the boat with poles, and a man at each end with a line on shore.

"Many a miner will die there," said Pete, when we were on our way again. We were well into the mountains by that time. They seemed to rise straight up from the banks of the river. It was a relief the next day to see the river broaden and the valley open up, even though we could hear the next set of rapids. Soon we could see the rocks sticking out with water foaming around them, but Pete had us out again, on the south bank this time, and he guided our canoes through with the lines.

We had to make a choice then. We could go to the right, up the Finlay, or to the left up the Parsnip. I knew that Cust and Carey's strike had been just a few miles along the Parsnip, so Black Jack and I decided to go that way. Pete and Joe decided on the Finlay. We had been panning every bar along the Peace and had found some colour. We all wanted a big find.

I should have known that Lady Luck would be waiting for Pete Toy. He was just that kind of man. Before the day was over he found a rich bar in the bank of the Finlay and he and Joe were soon taking out a dollar a pan, up to four hundred dollars a day in gold. Pete stayed there, and the river brought him new gold every day all summer long.

Black Jack and I didn't know about this at the time. We panned all along the Parsnip and ended up back in the Cariboo just as broke as ever. We learned about Pete's luck six years later when we came north again. We'd heard about more strikes, this time by Twelve Foot Davis, near the Omineca River that runs into the Finlay. We came up by Takla Lake and stayed around the strike for a year or so, trying out all the little streams.

Every time we met someone, we heard about Pete Toy. They all spoke of him with pleasure and talked about some kindness he'd done for them, like giving them grub or putting them up in a cabin when they were cold. You don't usually hear stories like that from miners. They all said that Pete was still making lots of money from his claim. He'd built a good solid cabin there on the Finlay and used it as a trading post. He'd spend the summer months working his claim, then travel to another cabin on the Parsnip for trapping, then across country to his winter cabin at Manson Creek west of the Forks for more trapping. People said that he was probably as rich from trapping as from gold. The country around there was full of game. He'd snowshoe or canoe down the Omineca in the spring to his cabin on the Finlay and then go on down the Peace to Fort St. John with his furs to get the goods for his trading post, and he'd make lots of purchases with gold dust.

I could tell that Black Jack was jealous. He had visions of doing that himself, buying things with gold dust. I couldn't help wondering myself, sometimes, why we hadn't turned north instead of south that day at the Forks. As I said, Pete Toy just seemed to have been born lucky.

Black Jack and I split up in the spring because, like a lot of other miners, I'd decided to spend a month or two down on the Peace. I figured my name should bring me some luck there. I had a chance to sit around a fire a few times again with Pete Toy as he was coming or going to Fort St. John. He was usually travelling with a partner or some friend. I would listen very carefully to their talk in case I could learn something more about finding gold. There was Dan Williams, who had one cabin at the Forks and another one across the river from Fort St. John. He made a good living panning gold on that long stretch of river between his cabins. He'd talk about what a fine garden he could grow on the banks of the Peace. Pete said Dan could shoot the eye out of a jackrabbit at a hundred yards if he wanted to.

Bill Cust, who'd found the first gold in those parts, would often be with Pete. He'd opened a trading post at the head of the portage, above the canyon, and did a good business. He even had the Hudson's Bay Company worried. The company had reopened a post where the old Portage House had been, across the river from the other end of the portage. They called it Hudson's Hope, and it was supposed to put Cust out of business.

One man I really liked was Jacques Pardonet. He was a good friend of Pete Toy's. He trapped and mined like Pete and was just about as strong, though he was shorter than most women, about five foot two. He had a big head and bushy hair and he liked to play a harmonica.

The other man I saw a few times was Henry Moberly. He was getting ready to leave the country. He'd been partners with Cust and Carey and had lived on the shores of that big lake south of the canyon. They used to call it White Fish Lake, but after Henry came they started calling it Moberly's Lake. Henry spoke as though there were thousands of fish and beaver and geese and swans at that lake and he'd had many fine hunts for caribou and moose and bear. It made me wonder if hunting wasn't a smarter way to earn a living than mining.

Yes, there were some nice times on the banks of the Peace that summer, with men talking around a fire and the night sky brightening up with the northern lights. You'd go to bed tired and then get up in the morning and see the snow shining on those twin peaks to the south and you'd be ready to get to work again, but even though I worked I didn't get much gold.

I thought my luck was finally going to change in the spring of 1871. I'd come back up the Omineca and was one of the first ones in to Germansen Creek when the big strike was made there. I went upstream with four other men and we washed out about four hundred ounces of gold in two weeks. We had to stop because of the high water. When we came back down we found a town already laid out and about a dozen houses being built. Men were arriving every day. It was strange to think of a town out there in the middle of those mountains. First there were five hundred men, then eight hundred. Then more gold was found about twelve miles away on Manson Creek, not far from Toy's winter cabin. Men can really work when there's gold involved. Before long there was a good trail built to Manson and hundreds more men arrived. There were four miles of claims staked along the creek, and the saloons and the poker games came too. I met up with Black Jack again as the men kept coming. By then there were no supplies for anybody and people were getting ugly. That's when I ran into Pete Toy.

Pete greeted me kindly with, "Hello, Peace River," but he said that Germansen Creek was the closest thing to civilization that he'd seen for ten years and he could hardly wait to get the dust of those streets off his boots. He was on his way to his winter cabin. He told me where it was, on the shore by the chain of lakes just beyond the gold strike.

When things slowed down in the winter, Black Jack suggested that we snowshoe in to Pete's cabin. Pete put us up for the night and made us a meal. He said that no man should try to talk on an empty stomach. It was the first time I'd seen him angry. He'd been out on his trapline and had seen two men sitting beside a cold campfire. He called out to them and when they didn't answer he went over and found that they were dead, frozen solid, probably starved. Pete said that he wished all this gold hunting would stop and that the country would just be left as it was.

"I've got all my gold hidden," he said. "I've no need for any of it."

I noticed that Black Jack paid attention to that.

Well, Pete's luck held, as usual. He didn't have to wait long for things to get back to normal. By the next summer the gold was petering out, except at Toy's Bar, and Germansen Creek had more houses than men. Black Jack and I went back along the Peace and earned a few dollars panning. There were sad-looking cabins here and there on the banks, built out of driftwood or logs. One had a flag above it, a sort of Union Jack, made out of overalls and flour sacks and parts of a red flannel shirt. People were pretty anxious to let any Americans who came along know that they were in a country owned by the British.

There had been hundreds of men who'd made claims along there. A lot hadn't survived. I heard about some who thought they could ride the rapids and were never seen again. Probably some bear dragged their bodies into the bush. I heard about some who went mad, they were so frightened of the solitude, especially in the pass, with the mountains all around them. I guess a few found a bit of gold and went back below the canyon and on to the south.

Black Jack and I often camped near the Forks. We would sit and talk about how different our lives could have been if it had been us, not Toy, who'd gone up the Finlay that day. Black Jack kept wondering where Pete had hidden his gold.

We were at the Forks when Pete came by in the fall. He'd hoped to see Dan Williams, but Dan was at Fort St. John. Pete stopped with us for a visit.

"Did you know that we're in part of Canada now?" he said. "I've just met a man called Hortensky. He said that British Columbia made a deal. They agreed to join the Confederation of Canada if a railway would be built to connect them to the east."

This was news to us, but it didn't make much difference. Politicians can't make gold.

But Pete kept talking.

"A railway across those prairies will be no problem, but trying to lay track through the Rocky Mountains will be tougher than finding a gold strike in these rivers."

We paid more attention when he mentioned gold again.

"This man Hortensky, he's been sent out by the government. He's been looking at that pass on the Peace to see if a railway could go there."

I could hardly imagine a train with people travelling through that valley. It would sure be different than paddling a canoe. Pete had more to say.

"Hortensky said it would be quite possible to put a road or a rail through there. So I told him about the other pass, the one I've heard about from Henry Moberly, that might even be easier."

There's Pete being helpful again, I thought. He'd told this Hortensky fellow how the Indians knew of a pass about thirty or forty miles south of the canyon. They could walk from Macleod's Lake to Hudson's Hope in four or five days. Pete called the pass the Pine River Pass.

What Pete said next was more interesting to us.

"Jacques Pardonet has struck it rich. He's taken three thousand dollars out of a bar on the Omineca."

That was something we needed to hear. We went back up to Germansen for the winter, played some cards, and waited for spring when we could do some more mining. We had been looking for gold for over eleven years and still hadn't found our fortune. We both felt that this was the year we'd be lucky.

In May we met Pardonet on the street in Germansen. He was guiding an important man called Major Butler who'd been sent out by the government. They'd tried to come up the Omineca when it was in full flood and had almost drowned. There's a canyon on that river, the Black Canyon, that's pretty bad—not nearly as bad as the one on the Peace, but at high water it's dangerous.

They had finally given up on the river and started to portage the canyon when they met Toy coming the other way. He had his canoe at the top of the portage and was planning to drop it down empty. They agreed to trade boats. Pete took their boat at the bottom of the canyon and went on to the Finlay, and Mr. Butler and Jacques carried their goods over the portage and came on up here in Pete's canoe. Pete had cooked them up a good meal before they left.

Jacques said that Mr. Butler had liked Pete and was going to write about him in his book. It sounded like Mr. Butler was quite an adventurer himself. He had come to Fort St. John by dog team and then to Hudson's Hope on horseback. He'd been lucky to find Jacques to help him on the river.

I knew that Pete must have been going to his claim and then on to Fort St. John. Black Jack kept wondering all the time where Pete had hidden his gold. He said one day that he was going to Manson Creek for a few card games. I knew there weren't many men there, so I was a little suspicious. I followed behind him and sure enough he turned off on the trail to Pete's cabin. There was quite a ruckus when he got there. I had to laugh. Pete's dogs were tied up outside and they made one holy noise when they smelled a stranger coming. Black Jack approached the cabin and opened the door. I knew then that he planned to rob Pete if he could find that gold. Then a frying pan came banging down on Black Jack's head and he left there howling louder than the dogs. He didn't know that Pete had a fine Indian wife who stayed at the cabin most of the summer.

Black Jack had quite a headache for a few days and I figured he had learned a lesson, so I didn't tell him I knew what had happened. I just kept marvelling to myself how Lady Luck stayed with Pete Toy.

Black Jack and I spent that summer on the Peace. We found some gold, just enough to buy what we needed at Cust's place. We split up again in the fall. I'd decided to winter at Hudson's Hope. Black Jack didn't tell me his plans. Next spring I headed up the Peace again, happy to be back on the river. I'd teamed up with Jacques Pardonet. I thought about Pete as we went through the Ne Parle Pas and the pass and the other rapids, then turned up the Finlay. Pete wasn't at his cabin, but the door was unlocked as always, and everything inside was neat as a pin.

We decided that Pete must be staying longer than usual at Manson. We went on to the Omineca and camped below the Black Canyon in the evening, ready to do the portage the next day. In the morning I heard Jacques yell.

"Peace River, look at that!" He pointed across the river. There was a battered canoe overturned on the bank. It looked like it might have been there all winter and was bobbing around now because of the high water.

"That's Pete's canoe," he said. "That's the one we traded him when I was with Mr. Butler."

There was no doubt in my mind that something terrible had happened. It looked like Lady Luck had finally abandoned Pete Toy.

We went on up to Germansen. There was no trace along the way of Pete's camp or gear or traps or anything. No one at Germansen had seen Pete all winter. They hadn't seen Black Jack Jones either. No one knew what had really happened.

I stayed on around the Peace. After all, where else should someone named Peace River Smith live? Sometimes, when I come safely through the Ne Parle Pas and I'm camped on shore with someone like Pardonet and there is a warm fire burning in front of us, I look up to watch the stars. Then the northern lights start dancing across the sky with all the colours of the rainbow, dancing in such a strange way that I think I see a man up there, a man so big and so strong that I know he can't be real. But I see him stepping out of a canoe, his blue eyes shining and his hand outstretched, ready to help any man. Then I wonder if Black Jack Jones is in a city somewhere, buying things with gold dust. Or maybe Pete Toy just stepped out of a canoe once too often. If that is what happened, maybe Lady Luck will find me now and show me where all that gold is hidden.

CHRONICLE

The traders and miners who stayed in the land of the Peace
proved that the white man could survive in the northern climate.
The parade of people on the river began to change. The travellers
who came were educated and they visited with a purpose. There
were engineers and surveyors, botanists and geologists, priests
and entrepreneurs. Most of them were sent by the government of
the new country of Canada to gather information about the
unknown miles of the northwest.

The first priority was to find a way through the Rockies for the
transcontinental railway. The search in the mountains was no
longer for gold, but for a suitable pass.

THE PINE RIVER PASS

1877

Joseph Hunter was discouraged. He sat alone in his tent and listened as the sounds of the camp drifted in to him from the outside. His dog Don, a red setter, sensed his mood and put his head on his master's knee.

Joseph stroked the dog's head and spoke to him. "The others are tired of travelling through these Rockies, Don, but we've yet to find the pass." Don thumped his tail as though he understood. Joseph kept his hand on the dog's head and thought about the struggle of the past few days, wondering to himself where he had gone wrong.

It had been over a week ago that they had stopped at Fort Macleod. No one there had known any details about a mountain pass that could be travelled on foot. The other route, through the Peace River Pass, was well documented. Hortensky had been through there, and Selwyn. The Peace Pass was low, at two thousand feet, and the snowfall was reported to be light, but the planners for the railway were not convinced that the route should be so far north. Rumours of the Pine River Pass, south of the Peace, had to be investigated.

Selwyn had searched. He had gone east from the Parsnip without success and then, from the other side of the Rockies, had followed the Pine upstream from the Peace. He had reached a point where the Pine was joined by another river from the south. He had even climbed a high hill that he said was flat as a table at the top. He had seen the mountains on the western horizon from there, but no sign of a pass. Now he, Joseph Hunter, had been sent to search the Rockies, and things were not going well. Perhaps he had been wrong to believe the Indian woman.

Joseph's meeting with the woman had been very strange. It had happened at Fort Macleod when he was out looking for Don. The dog, who usually never left his side, had gone missing. Joseph found him on the shore of the lake, sitting beside the woman. She looked out over the water, watching the lake absorb the colours of the setting sun. A solitary loon swam on the water in front of her.

Don had not moved as Joseph approached. The woman had turned and beckoned to Joseph. He noticed her dark hair streaked with white, and the necklace of white beads that she wore over her dark dress. She spoke only three words. "I'll show you," she said. She had taken a stick and drawn a map in the sand. She marked the Misinchinka River and then the mountains. She indicated that the Misinchinka was the river he must follow to find the pass. There had been something about the way the dog accepted the woman that made Joseph think he should believe her. Don was always a good judge of people. Joseph had heard the call of the loon echo across the lake as he returned to the Fort with the dog.

In the morning Joseph had directed his party to follow the Misinchinka, as the woman had suggested. They followed the river for days, through bramble and bush and fallen trees, and ended up surrounded by mountains. Joseph had even climbed to the top of one of the mountains. He found alpine violets, and Don had a good romp in the snow, but there was no sign of a depression in the Rocky barrier to the south that might be a pass. To the north, though, there was a suggestion of one low break in the mountain range. He had returned to camp and directed the party to travel in that direction. They followed a stream, the Atunatche, that was a branch of the Misinchinka, and it led them to the meadow where they were now camped. There was still no evidence of a pass. The woman must have been wrong.

The camp had become quiet as Joseph reviewed the journey in his mind. The evening light would soon begin to fade.

"I guess we should turn back, Don," he said to the dog.

Don raised his head as if to ask a question. The dog stood up and moved to the door of the tent. He began to pace back and forth.

"What do you hear, boy?" asked Joseph, as he undid the tent flap. He stepped outside with the dog beside him. He expected to hear a bear snorting around the camp, or the faint howl of a wolf. Instead he heard a call, like the cry of an old woman or the laugh of a crazy man. It was a distant yodel, trembling through the trees. Joseph smiled and crouched beside Don. He put his arm around the dog. "Don," he said, "that's the sound of a loon. There has to be a lake nearby. A lake may mean a summit, a summit means a pass."

In the morning, Joseph, with two other men, left the rest of the party at camp and rode north, with Don following along. Before noon they reached a lake. The water was jade green and reflected the steep mountains along the far shore. Beyond the shadow of the mountains swam a pair of loons.

The men followed the closest lakeshore and found a stream leading northwest and then east. Beyond, stretching towards the Peace, lay the valley they had been seeking. Joseph Hunter had been shown the way to the Pine River Pass.

CHRONICLE

Two years later, in 1879, another railway survey party came from the west to visit the land of the Peace. The group divided into two at Macleod Lake. One section travelled by river down the Parsnip and the Peace, through the Peace Pass. The second went on horseback through the Pine Pass, using a mule train of almost one hundred animals to carry their goods. They were led by the geologist Dr. George Dawson,[3] a man who later wrote enthusiastic reports about the climate of the area and the fertility of the land.

Decisions were made far away about the route of the railway. Neither the Peace Pass nor the Pine Pass were used. The railway project was completed in 1885, using the Kicking Horse Pass far to the south.

During this time, buildings other than trading posts began to appear in some locations along the river as missions were established.

3   See note on page 155.

AT AN ANGLICAN
MISSION ON THE PEACE[4]

1888

Dear Margaret;

Your letter arrived! What a pleasure! You have no idea how I enjoyed reading the many pages, as it is very seldom that I am able to have a visit with another woman. James, of course, is fine company, and I am learning a few words of the Beaver dialect so that I can talk to the families camped nearby, but the long, dark evenings of winter are sometimes lonely. I often think of the times, so long ago, when we played together as children, innocently promising to be friends forever. Little did we know that fate would have us separated by an ocean and most of a continent!

Yes, our journey here was strenuous. I hope I did not sound too full of complaints in my letter. I have to keep reminding myself that those who came before us did not even have the luxury of train and stage as far as Edmonton. They came the entire way by rivers and lakes and old Indian trails. The roads beyond Edmonton are now wide enough for oxen and carts, and York boats and rafts are available for travel on the water. With almost four hundred of those miles to cover, however, I did wonder a few times if all my precious belongings would float away down some unnamed stream. Of

---

4 See note on page 155.

course we always had the excitement of wondering what was ahead, to offset the roughness of the journey.

We are finding that our mission work is much needed and I am kept busy with duties in the house, chapel, and schoolroom. As I mentioned, we have native families, mostly of the Beaver tribe, nearby. These people are gentle and shy, and James has made great progress in learning their language. You may have heard of other Anglican missions in the north, in particular the work of Bishop Bompas. He followed the Peace River as far as the mountains a number of years ago and doubtless saved many lives by doing smallpox vaccinations. Strangely enough, our Anglican mission work blends well with the work done by the Roman Catholic priests. They have travelled the north and established missions up and down the river routes for many years. Somehow the vastness of these regions makes our differences less important.

I must tell you that the flower seeds that Mother had tucked in with my linens did grow, and I have never been so happy in all my life to see some familiar blossoms. There have been vegetable gardens and grains such as barley planted here before, with great success, but not flowers. The soil is rich in the river valley and the summer days are long and bright. There is much controversy over whether the region beyond the river will ever be suitable for agriculture. They say that there is sometimes frost in July!

So you were amused by the thought of me trying to maintain my decorum while bouncing and swaying around in a wagon on rough trails! You will find it even more hilarious to imagine me chasing a moose out of my garden! Fortunately, James heard the commotion and came out with his gun. Did you know that a roast of moose is delicious?

What a coincidence that your Uncle Joseph also knew this river. I remember when your Father received that one letter from him. I thought at the time how adventurous his life sounded, especially since he claimed to have found a lot of gold. I recall your father dismissing his brother as a dreamer who had to follow new trails. I don't suppose you will ever know what became of him or his treasure. There are still two or three men of that gold mining era who stop here at the trading post. They seem to be a type, like your Uncle, who prefer to live at the very edge of civilization. Although they visit the trading post, they seem uncomfortable near our mission. They are rough men, but generous. One of them had grown a fine garden at Fort St. John and he brought me some potatoes for planting. I asked if he recalled your Uncle and he answered yes, that your Uncle Joseph had prospected with someone named Pete Toy.

I must close, but will so look forward to your next letter. I do want to keep up on all your family news. We will soon have a little one of our own to cherish, perhaps before this letter reaches you.

Your very good friend,

Catherine

A VOICE NEAR THE TRADING POST

1889

Did you hear about the lady
At the mission over there?
I saw her just this evening
As she joined her man in prayer.

She's all the way from England
And she's careful how she looks.
Her husband is the Reverend
And he teaches from his books.

They stood beside a tiny grave
And held each other's hand.
I did not know what words to say
That they would understand.

And so I rang their mission bell
And hoped that holy sound
Would help their babe to rest in peace
Beneath that fresh dug ground.

CHRONICLE

In 1897 the excitement of the Klondike gold rush reached the
Peace as hopeful miners travelled north on an all-Canadian route.
Some followed the trail from Edmonton which had been
established by Inspector Moodie of the North West Mounted
Police. Others came over the old Cariboo trail and on through the
Pine Pass. Very few of the adventurers who began the journey
ever reached the Yukon. Many turned back, many died, and a few
remained in the Peace as pioneers. The influx of large numbers of
often unruly people was resented by the local population.

A DREAMER SPEAKS

1897

I stand on a hill
to see in all ways
and hear the hunters' guns.
The buffalo trails are empty
and shaggy bulls
no longer drink
the river.
Even the beaver hide
as men
come
like wolves
to destroy the moose and deer.
They do not hear
our angry
silence.

THE BALLAD OF GRAVEYARD CREEK

1899

The graves are washed by summer rain
The graves are wet and cold
The graves of men who travelled north
In search of Yukon gold.

Two thousand men went up the trail
They left from Edmonton
They went to seek a fortune but
Most found oblivion.

These twenty men who travelled north
So they'd be rich some day
Had planned to reach Bonanza Creek
But they got just halfway.

Now twenty graves are near the creek
And twenty markers plain
And twenty names are known no more
And won't be known again.

So who sleeps here beneath this grass
And why did these men die?
Who marked the graves with slabs of wood
And built a fence nearby?

How many more died in the cold
How many more were drowned
How many wandered without food
Were lost and never found?

For many men walked near the Peace
As fortunes they did seek
Now twenty men sleep 'neath the grass
That grows at Graveyard Creek.

The graves hide under winter snow
The graves are wet and cold
The graves of men who travelled north
In search of Klondike gold.

CHRONICLE

The gold rush to the Klondike ended, and some of the surviving men, who had not gone beyond the Peace, decided to remain. Farther away, the railway brought change to the west. The prairie land filled with settlers, and towns and cities took shape. The land of the Peace, without a railway, remained unchanged, and the Peace River was the only highway of the northwest. It was seen by very few, but as the travellers on the river wrote reports and books, people all over the country heard about this unknown river and land.

THE POOR MAN'S COUNTRY

1903

(The voice of biologist James Macoun, son of Professor John Macoun)

It is a rain-infested land
of muskeg and swamp,
useless and harsh.
Why, frost comes in every month
and even the hardy starve.
Winter at sixty below
is fit for no man.
Only those who have little
and will settle for less
should consider
living
in the land of the Peace.

A JOURNEY DOWN THE PEACE RIVER

October 1906

a special report to the *Edmonton Bulletin*
by William Adamson

I am writing to your newspaper, as you suggested, with an account of my recent journey down the great river of the north, the Peace.

The journey began at Fort Macleod. This establishment is a collection of log buildings that does business with the local people in the village nearby. It is situated on a long lake where we launched our canoes. We traveled the length of the lake and continued on through Tudja Lake and the Pack River to reach the Parsnip. This river is as ordinary as its name, which comes from the strange plant growing on its banks. We passed, on our left, the river known as the Nation. Readers will have heard about this river if they read Mr. Pike's account of his terrible adventure there. He mistook the Nation for the Pack and became hopelessly lost in early winter trying to reach Fort Macleod. He was near starvation as he retraced his steps to the canyon, and had to resort to boiling up strips of moose hide, intended as repair material for his moccasins, to stay alive.

The Parsnip widens considerably where it joins the Finlay to become the Peace. The distance across is at least half a mile. A few miles north of the junction is the bar where the legendary Mr. Toy found his gold. There are still rumours of nuggets of gold waiting there to be found. We did not visit that area but followed the river to the east.

The location of the Finlay Forks has tremendous potential. To the west is a large level plain suitable for buildings, and the entire area is surrounded by an amphitheatre of mountains. I expect that some day there will be a large city there.

Rapids can be heard from the fork of the river. These are called the Finlay Rapids even though they are located on the first few miles of the Peace.

We had no trouble with the rapids as we unloaded the boats and lined them through. We were into the pass almost immediately and the river narrowed to a width of two hundred and fifty feet. The mountain that forms the southern base of the pass has been named Mt. Selwyn in honour of Mr. Selwyn, whose reports have been widely published. He determined that this pass was definitely in the Rocky Mountains and that the canyon of rocks at the portage was not. Mt. Selwyn is described as a mountain of quartz and I'm sure it will have commercial value as soon as transportation becomes available. The scenery will then become known all over the world for its unsurpassed grandeur.

When we were through the pass we spent one delightful evening fishing in a deep pool near the mouth of the Clearwater River, where it joins the Peace. The trout were voracious and easily caught by dangling bait on a line.

We then passed over the Ne-Parle-Pas Rapids, which are well named. The water there moves with sinister smoothness, but our passage was uneventful because of our experienced crew. Beyond the rapids the river winds with a steady current through the foothills in a mile-wide valley, the width of the water being three to four hundred feet. This was a very pleasant part of the journey. When looking east you can see the original passageway of the river, which is now the portage route. It is a natural valley between two large foothills. The southern hill was named Portage Mountain by Mr. Selwyn. It forms the northern base of the twenty-mile canyon that is the present tortuous path of the river. The northern hill has been called Bullhead Mountain for many years, a quaint name referring to the whitened skull of a buffalo that marked a camping place on the portage. It was said to be the skull of the last buffalo killed in the area.

These two hills are the southern spur of what has been named Butler Ridge, in recognition of the author of that wonderful and well-known story of adventure entitled "The Wild North Land." The ridge was a pretty sight, covered with golden poplar and capped with snow.

The speed of the river increases as it approaches the canyon, and the water widens to give the appearance of a lake. The banks on the north have been undercut by the water swirling to the right to enter the canyon. We could hardly hear our own voices above the roar of the river as we unloaded at the portage.

The boats were left near the remnants of Cust's House, to be picked up by the crew on their return trip. Pack horses were available where the portage trail begins. There are immense heaps of sand and gravel along this trail, and travel is up and down from one terrace to another. There are stretches of tall poplars and spruce and some burned areas. There is no sight of the river all along the fourteen miles of the portage.

The trail ends at Hudson's Hope. This post used to be across the river, just beyond the lower end of the canyon. There are four buildings at the present location. Two belong to the Hudson's Bay Company and two to the rival Revillon Frères.

The view from the post is spectacular, as you can see many miles downstream and also south toward Moberly's Lake. Commerce will certainly come to this site in the future. The canyon will no doubt be dammed to provide power for huge industries, and rumours are that the coal nearby is of the highest quality. Railways will likely branch in all directions.

The first sternwheeler had recently reached the Hope, so the days of the canoe and barge may soon be over. I was able to arrange passage on this vessel, a Hudson's Bay Company boat named the *Peace River*. I took advantage of the few days waiting time to cross the river and follow the trail to Moberly's Lake. I was able to meet one of the area's legends in the person of a man named Baptiste. He is of Iroquois heritage and is a renowned hunter. It is said that he can walk through the coldest of winter snow without socks in his moccasins and have no discomfort, the snow melting in his tracks.

I enjoyed the relative comfort of the sternwheeler when I resumed my journey. I had taken time before our departure to examine the strange islands that are present in the river near Hudson's Hope. Being a journalist and not a scientist, I cannot speculate by what force of nature these were created. They are as high as the surrounding hills and are topped with a growth of trees. They guard the beginnings of the canyon, which I did not attempt to investigate as there are many stories of those who have met their death in the treacherous waters within those walls. The most recent concerned a party of two who attempted to run the canyon from above and were never heard of again.

The river east of the canyon passes between terraced hills that are some eight hundred feet high. The southern banks are wooded, while the northern slopes are grassy. There is a trail along the north shore, but no sign of a house or building until Fort St. John.

Stopping at this fort was a most interesting experience, and the activity there was a contrast to the quiet days we had known on the river. The fort, on the north shore at the foot of a high bank, has been relocated several times. The last site, fifty years ago, was across the river.

Inspector Moodie of the North West Mounted Police was present at the fort. His crew was continuing work on the trail to the Yukon. Surveyors from the Grand Trunk Railway were there as well, en route to the Pine Pass. The provincial mineralogist was compiling information about the vast mineral resources of the area, and the Roman Catholic priest was at the Mission. In addition, there was the Hudson's Bay Company staff under the agent Mr. Frank Beaton, and the men of the Revillon Frères. The gardens at these establishments, incidentally, were impressive.

The most significant presence at the fort this past summer was that of Mr. J. A. Macdonell. As most readers will know, the whole of the Peace country between the Rockies and the B.C. border has been held in a special Government reserve as part of the agreement reached regarding the railway when B.C. became the sixth province of Confederation. Mr. Macdonell had recently finished the survey of the three and one-half million acres due the Federal Government. Perhaps when the boundaries of this Peace River Block are known, the area will be opened for homesteading. With the prairie land along the railways to the south filling with settlers, this new land will bring a necessary breadth to our country.

Two other men at the fort were of interest. One, Mr. A.M. Bezanson, can be truly called a land prospector. He is enthusiastic about the future of the area and I predict he will be a promoter. The other, Mr. Hector Tremblay, was acting as a guide for Mr. Macdonell. Mr. Tremblay recently cut a trail south from here to the Pouce Coupe prairie which Dr. Dawson described so well. Mr. Tremblay hopes to settle in that area as he feels the agricultural potential is enormous.

I will complete my account of Fort St. John by referring to the events that happened here before Treaty 8 was signed. The Beaver are known for their honesty and integrity and they resented, with good reason, the behaviour of some of the Klondikers who passed this way. Ponies, caches of food, snowshoes, etc., were stolen by the prospectors, and the traps and snares belonging to the natives were sometimes deliberately damaged. Five hundred of the Beaver people gathered together and prevented the entry of the travellers into these Indian hunting grounds until there was a guarantee of the treaty.

After leaving Fort St. John, we were soon beyond the Peace River Block and were travelling within the boundaries of the new province of Alberta. We reached Dunvegan and then Peace River Crossing without incident. The river valley along the way varies in width from four hundred to a thousand yards, and the river, at a width that I estimate to be three hundred feet, creates sandbars and drift piles as it curves along. The sandbars are a navigational problem in the fall to a boat such as the *Peace River*.

Readers are no doubt familiar with the reports by Mr. Hortensky, Mr. John Macoun, and others, who describe this area all along the Peace River as the future garden of the west, with a climate similar to Belleville, Ontario. I was told that chinook winds make the winters quite bearable.

There are reports of a huge fertile prairie south of Dunvegan. Farming has already been proven successful by a Mr. Lawrence farther north at Fort Vermilion.

I left the river at Peace River Crossing, near the point where the Smoky joins the Peace. As I prepared to leave for Edmonton, I sat on my horse and surveyed the valley from the high banks above the river. I could not help being awed by the realization that I had travelled over a route taken by many famous men and that I was, right then, near an historic spot. The Beaver and Cree met near there, long ago, to give the river the beautiful name of Unchaga, River of Peace, and Alexander Mackenzie wintered near that location before his remarkable journey to the Pacific.

I hope my account will give readers some understanding of the riches that wait to be discovered in the land of the Peace. I can only summarize by naming the country the Land of Tomorrow.

THE TRAILS LEAD NORTH

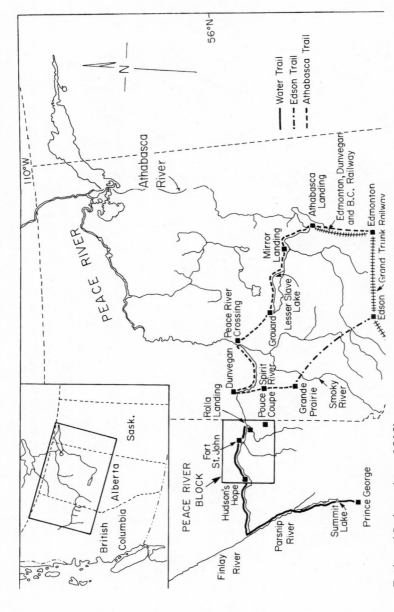

Trails and Railways (circa 1913)

A DREAMER SPEAKS

1908

People of the rapids[5]
have come from the east
to live by the lake.
We will blend
with them
for they know
like us
the spirits of the peaks.

---

5   See note on page 155.

THE BULL OUTFIT [6]

1909

We had fine farms
in Ontario
but our church said we were wrong,
heretics,
living without dogma.
Our dreams
were of freedom for our faith.
We heard God's word
and came west
by train
with our plows and stoves
and other things.
In Edmonton
we asked about the north.
"Take the Long Trail,"
they said.
"Find the valley of the Beaverlodge River
and you will be home."
We bought wagons
and oxen
and wondered if it was wise
to use beasts with cloven hooves.
Thirty-one souls
began the journey
and our eighteen teams,

---

6   See note on page 155.

strong and broad,
gave our outfit the name of Bull.
The devil was not in the beasts
but in the muskeg
and the mud.
At Athabasca
tons of our goods were shipped
on the river
but we,
with the oxen,
laboured on the trail.
We slid down the icy hills
and the still-loaded wagons
sank axle deep
in gullies of mud
'til we made corduroy paths of logs.
The rivers led
to Lesser Slave Lake
where steamboat passage for the women
was bought
by the men cutting cords of wood for the fuel,
before they followed the rocky lakeshore west.
Finally,
Grouard, almost a town,
with mission and post,
then more miles of trail
for everything and everyone
to reach Peace River Crossing.
Here, the vista
to the west,
where rivers met and lilies bloomed,
gave some hope
that our home might yet be found.
We crossed the sweeping river

to follow the trail to Dunvegan
hoping we might see farms along the way.
Again we crossed the Peace
to find mosquitoes
and a trail going south.
We passed Spirit River
and went over the Saddle Hills
to the lake called Saskatoon.
Wild berries waited
and mountains gleamed
in the distance.
We chose our homesteads
and gave thanks for the fire
that twelve years before
had cleared the land
leaving burned timber
for our log homes.
Eighty-three days
it had been
and five hundred miles or more
living with wagons and oxen
and aching hands
on our Long Trail journey
to the valley where freedom was.

THE STORY OF TOM AND HARRY

1910

It is not the frozen river
That makes the blood run cold,
It's the fever in the cabins
And the stories that are told
Of those so bushed in wintertime
They know not what they do.
This is such a story.
They say that it is true.

Two trappers shared a cabin
In the season of the snow.
The mercury was dropping,
Reaching thirty-nine below.
Tom took out his hammer,
Started pounding nails.
Harry said that it was time
To check the trapping trails

Tom kept up the pounding
In the cabin by the Peace.
Harry yelled at Tom and said,
"That hammering must cease."
The argument continued
As the men went out the door.
It seemed the river's name was
No longer Peace but War.

Harry found his rifle
And aimed it at his friend.
He threatened him with death and said,
"Your money I will spend."
But the gun was never fired
For a hammer hit his head.
Harry made the threat, but
Was on the ground, quite dead.

The one policeman in the land
Soon came riding by.
He saw the frozen corpse and said,
"This case the courts must try."
He rounded up the man named Tom
And put him on a horse.
"We'll go to see the judge," he said,
"With evidence, of course."

The judge was many miles away.
The corpse too big to carry.
The officer picked up an ax
And took the head off Harry.
The head went in a bucket
And the bucket in a sack,
And with the lone policeman
It went on his horse's back.

The strange procession reached the judge.
The lawman told the tale.
Tom listened for the verdict
As the lawman raised the pail
And emptied out the frozen head
Onto the courtroom desk.
The frozen bits of blood and bone
Made Harry look grotesque.

The judge's voice was shaky.
"Well, such evidence is rare.
But why did you threaten your partner?"
He said to the head lying there.
That is the end of the story
For Tom was free to go.
He travelled with the lawman
Back to the land of snow.

So remember how the fever
That burns in winter's cold
Can reach the frozen river
And destroy the brave and bold.
For when nights are dark and lonely
A soul can darken too
And there is no way of knowing
What such a soul will do.

CHRONICLE

The river kept moving regardless of what happened nearby. It rolled the strength of its water over the Finlay Rapids while a few buildings were built at the Forks. It passed swiftly through the Rockies as it always had and silenced its strength in the Ne Parle Pas Rapids. It moved quickly along the valley of the foothills, unaffected by the few people who claimed land along its shores. The terrible force of its water tumbled through the rocky passageway of the canyon, unchanged by the men who dreamed of mining the seams of coal along the way. It continued to provide passage for a few canoes and steamships as it stretched eastwards through the plains. It remained the only transportation route in the land.

The mystique of the north, which had developed during the days of the Klondike gold rush, was transferred to the mid-north, and the land of the Peace became the land of promise. The Alberta sections, being more accessible, were settled first. In 1912 the Canadian government opened the Peace River Block to homesteading. The search by adventurers was no longer for furs or gold. The rush was on for the fertile acres of land in the region.

The river and two rough trails were the only connections between the Peace area and the southern parts of British Columbia and Alberta. Settlers and promoters began arriving, using these routes. They came down river by barge from central B.C. They came from Edmonton by horse or oxen and cart over the old Athabasca Trail. They walked or rode over the newly constructed Edson Trail. The settlers knew that the future of the region depended on a rail connection to the south and they were excited by rumours of railways to be built. The railway was expected to reach the Pouce Coupe prairie from Edmonton. It was to extend to Peace River Crossing and Hudson's Hope. Rail from Vancouver was expected through the Peace or Pine Pass. There were even plans for a railway that would go up the Finlay Valley to Alaska. Rumour after rumour was heard and land booms developed at Hudson's Hope and Pouce Coupe. Suddenly there were forty people living at Hudson's Hope and another thirty lived along the river between there and Fort St. John. Four hundred people were in the area of Pouce Coupe and others settled at Swan Lake and Rolla. Someone new, on foot or horseback, arrived every day in the new town of Grande Prairie to look the country over. The land of the Peace was a land of bright dreams.

THE LAST WEST[7]

1912

I read it in the paper,
so it is true.
An empty land
waits in the Peace,
an Eden,
spread like a park
over millions of acres,
dotted with brush,
rolling towards the mountains
for hundreds of miles,
a Grande Prairie, a Little Prairie,
and others in between,
all, ready for the plow.
Why, the grass is as high as a horse's belly
and potatoes grow to be the size of turnips.
I saw the picture,
so it is true,
cabbage and cauliflower,
squash and pumpkin,
cucumbers and tomatoes,
all this and more
to sow
and grow
in this land of Canaan.
The soil,

---

7   See note on page 155.

rich and dark, the bed of an ancient lake,
is waiting
for oats and barley and wheat,
that can ripen in the long hours
of summer light
and be bathed at night
by gentle rain.
Aspen and willow
timbered hills
lakes and creeks and rivers,
why, nothing is lacking.
I read it, so it is true.
It is the Promised Land
with
game to hunt
berries to pick
fish to catch
furs to trap,
a land
waiting for homesteaders,
a land
that will feed a million people.
I am restless and must move on
to this Eldorado.
I will ride to the end of the steel,
then follow a northern trail
to the Peace,
the last frontier,
where the silent, empty land
I read about
is waiting.

NEAR FINLAY FORKS [8]

1913

Lucy left the path and walked towards the river. The sun was low in the sky and the outline of Mt. Selwyn to the east was darkening. She could hear the rapids in the distance. How long would it be, she wondered, until John came home. Probably one or two weeks.

It was her first experience with autumn in this north country. In California, it would still be hot and the hills would be golden brown. Here, the air was crisp and cool, and the leaves of the cranberry bushes were turning red.

The rounded stones rolled underfoot as she walked closer to the water. It was huge, this Peace River, and it beckoned one to travel. John had wanted her to go with him for the winter supplies and maybe stay out, at least until the baby was born. But the cabin was their home now and that's where she wanted to be. Three hundred miles of travel by canoe sounded worse than being alone right now. And she wasn't totally alone. Annie came every day with some of her children. Lucy knew that Annie was watchful because of the pregnancy, and curious that a white woman would come and stay in this land. Annie had six children, all healthy and tumbling about like little bear cubs. Their father ran the trading post at Finlay Forks. Annie, with her round, pretty face and her shy smile, would be her midwife in two months time, when the baby was due.

Lucy looked back up the trail. The bench above, where the cabin was located, gave a magnificent view. The river valley, extending beyond Mt. Selwyn, led downstream to the canyon. Upstream, where the two rivers met to form the Peace, was the trading post. It was sure to be a centre of commerce in the future, as the twentieth century unfolded. But she liked it best here, beside the river, where she could be refreshed by the sounds of the moving water. She would soon have to think of a name for their new home.

The air became cool as the sun slipped behind the mountains to the west. Lucy crossed the river flat to go back to the trail. She was tired. She had been pulling roots all day, preparing a garden patch. She would have a cup of tea when she reached the cabin. She stopped suddenly as she heard a man's shout. It was John's loud halloo.

All's well, she thought as she waved and ran towards the river. I will call our home *All's Well*.

CHRONICLE

Once again, events beyond the river determined what would happen in the land of the Peace. World War I broke out in Europe and Canada went to war. Railway plans for the northwest were no longer a priority, and men who had planned to be settlers joined the army and went overseas. The railway extended from Edmonton to Peace River Crossing in 1915. The following year it reached Spirit River. The grade was completed from there to the B.C. border, but the plan for a Pouce Coupe destination was abandoned and a connection was made to Grande Prairie. The land in the Peace remained unchanged and the river flowed on past cabins that were deserted.

THE TALK IN FRANCE
OF NORTHERN TRAILS

1917

Oh, I remember the Edson Trail
I walked before the war.
It took me through the muskeg
And I walked ten days or more
'Til I found the fertile farmland
With a beaver lodge nearby,
But until this war is over
It's my homestead dreams that die.

The Old Trail, the Long Trail
Is being changed to steel.
No more the broken axle
On the groaning wagon wheel.
No icy sleighs in winter time,
No horses falling down,
When you travel to the north now
Past Athabasca town.

My trail was made of water
And I left from Summit Lake.
I followed all the rivers
And portages had to take.
I reached the Rolla Landing
And walked beyond a bit
And that's where I'll go back to
When this army I can quit.

RETURN TO THE PEACE

October 1926

a special report to the *Edmonton Bulletin*
by William Adamson

Twenty years ago I made a trip down the Peace River and wrote a report about the experience. I recently travelled on the river for a second time and I would like to tell your readers what changes there have been.

This trip was shorter than the one in 1906 as I left from Edmonton and went only as far as Hudson's Hope. The journey was simpler, as well, because of the changes in transportation. I was able to take the train to the settlement of Peace River and then board the sternwheeler, the *D.A. Thomas*. This boat is fitted with staterooms, a dining room, and a ballroom, and it can accommodate over one hundred passengers.

The trip to Hudson's Hope can be made in seventeen hours, but the travel time is usually several days because there are many stops along the way. Fuel must be picked up and goods are loaded and unloaded. Settlers are contracted at certain landings to supply wood for fuel. This wood is piled in four-foot lengths and tossed onto the deck from a ramp on the river bank. Stops are made at other locations if a cloth is hanging from a stick on shore.

A comfortable sternwheeler travelling on the Peace River is an unexpected convenience. It is also a surprise to see the captain of the boat using a rifle. The captain explained with a smile that a moose or bear on a hillside could easily jump in the river and attack the boat! Hunting is a popular sport in the region and we frequently saw game along the river banks.

The boat was built to fulfill the dreams of Lord Rhonda, who planned to develop the coal fields near Hudson's Hope. The *D.A. Thomas* was originally fitted with oil tanks in the hope that oil would be discovered in the surrounding countryside. The boat traffic on the Peace River was to connect with rail traffic across the north. It was to link the Pacific coast at Kitimat with Prince Albert, Saskatchewan. The Great War put an end to these dreams and the boat was purchased two years ago by the Hudson's Bay Company.

The Great War has had another effect on the Peace country as the area has attracted many veterans. Some had visited before the war, while others were looking not for furs or gold, as adventurers of the past had done, but for the promise of peace that they heard in the name of the river. It is true that as you travel along this river with only the sounds of the boat to disturb the silence, you do wonder why there were battles such as those at Vimy Ridge and Passchendaele. Soldier settlement schemes also brought in many veterans, as the prospects for successful farming in the area are exceptional.

I understand that the lack of rail transportation is a serious problem for settlers. One of our stops was at Rolla Landing, where we heard about the fine crops produced a few miles to the south. Oats and wheat from this region won the top prizes at the recent International Grain Show in Chicago. I was told that oats produce fifty to one hundred bushels to the acre and wheat at least forty. Unfortunately, there is no easy way of getting this produce to market. The grain has to be freighted seventy miles in the cold of winter to the railway at Spirit River. Ironically, the freight route, which is too boggy to use at other times of the year, is the grade that was built ten years ago for a railway that didn't arrive. It is not surprising that local people have been asking for a tenth province in Canada, the province of Peace River.

The river and scenery are, of course, unchanged since I was last here, but other things have altered. Almost every craft on the river, except for the sternwheeler, is now using a gasoline engine. The fort of Dunvegan is no longer in operation, and settlers' cabins are seen occasionally along the river banks. A ferry is available at Taylor Flats, west of Rolla Landing. Fort St. John is now a settlement and has been relocated farther north on a plateau above the river. There are also ranches near the Halfway River and Hudson's Hope. The snow-covered peaks on the western horizon, however, are constant and remain spectacular.

The arrival of the *D.A. Thomas* at Hudson's Hope was a social event for the settlement, and most of the residents came aboard for a dinner and dance. This gave me an opportunity to talk to several people, including the young man who takes the mail on to Finlay Forks and Fort Graham.

He told me that there are still people making a living washing for gold on the upper Peace. He also described two homes on the river above the canyon. One is a log home, called *All's Well*, which even has an organ. The other is at the very successful Beattie ranch. The Beattie family maintains a truck road over the old portage route.

The Peace River Canyon at Hudson's Hope remains unconquered. Many people have described the river's huge power potential. Coal is being mined in the canyon at present. The seam is eight feet thick and of the highest quality. The mine is just a few miles beyond the point where Alexander Mackenzie hauled out his canoe.

Even more amazing than the stories of the region's coal and power potential are the reports of footprints in the shale near the coal mine. The imprints have been made by some prehistoric beast. They are six inches deep, have three toes, and measure over three and one-half feet in length. There are also reports of a fossilized skeleton in the river bank below the Ne Parle Pas Rapids. These remains are from a type of marine reptile. Some day we may understand more about these things.

There was a lot of laughter during the evening while we were docked at Hudson's Hope. Mr. Gething, the owner of the mine, talked about the last visit of the *D.A. Thomas.* Mr. Gething had apparently persuaded the captain to try to navigate the canyon with the sternwheeler and the boat had almost met with disaster. The one-hundred-and-sixty-foot steamer was no more successful than Mackenzie's canoe had been. The story is an example of how the spirits of the early explorers are still present among those who live and work on the Peace.

My return to Peace River and Edmonton was uneventful and my enthusiasm for the future of this region is as unchanged as the river. If I was still a young man, I would be joining the many others who are moving norththward to homestead.

FROM ROLLA TO
THE SPIRIT RIVER RAILHEAD[9]

1927

Shadows lengthen in the white woods
as we plod
with the horses
breath steaming
at twenty below.
Sleighs glide
with singing runners,
the only steel this trail will know.
Golden grain,
full of summer's sun,
a precious, creaking cargo
to sell.
Soon, a lantern,
swinging in the gathering dark
will tell
of shelter
barn and bunkhouse
and thoughts of home.
Two more days
of mittened hands
and muffled ears
and horses,
poor creatures,
hooked up, four to a load.

---

9   See note on page 155.

Jingling harness
will sound the way
until we hear the whistle of the train.
Then back the many miles
to come again
and again
on this tree-lined trail
where the shadows lengthen
in the white woods.

THE SIMPLE LIFE

1928

So you're the new man on the mail route? Well, sit down at the table and rest yourself. Yes, they call me Boom. That's right, I've been around a few years. Settled here after the war when there was nothing to see but a trail through the bush. Did you see that stream outside and those big spruce trees? When I first saw those I filed on a homestead and stayed right here; cut the logs to make this cabin and cleared some land out back to grow oats for the horse, and with a garden and a few chickens, I figured I had everything I'd ever need. Well, sure, I had to argue with the bears now and then about who owned this place, but other than that, life has been pretty simple.

That's a good job you've got, carrying the mail. Well, my life gets busy too, even if it is simple. You can't have a house by the side of a road and not be busy. People on the trail started stopping by after I moved in, and word soon got around that I was a good cook. Folks who were travelling, like you, always aimed to get here at meal time. Before I knew it I was running a stopping place. Had to build a bunkhouse, too, so folks could stay over if the weather got bad.

Yes, Boom is a funny name. Some of the other bachelors around here started calling me that when I told them how I used my shotgun to chase the bears away from my turnips. None of them could understand why I was doing all that shooting without killing any bears. Boom, boom, boom, they'd say to me. But, you know, some of those bears got to be like old friends, coming around every fall. There was one old black one I could always expect. I'd yell and holler at him that this was my place and I didn't want any company and then I'd shoot a couple of shots off into the air and away he'd go. One year he got too smart and got in with the chickens, so I had to kill him. I felt kind of bad about that. I made him into that rug on the floor over there. There wasn't any choice about killing him. I have to have my chickens because I never know who'll come by next for a meal. I always keep at least one chicken ready for the pan and a pie or two on hand. Sure, I make a few dollars running this place, but I'd never let someone go hungry if they couldn't pay.

Of course I like living here. I don't suppose I could sleep at night if I couldn't hear something howling, like the wolves or the coyotes or the wind. I like to hear folks talk to each other, too, when they stop by. I'm not much on talking myself and it's mighty entertaining to hear one person trying to outdo the other. I expect things are a bit exaggerated at times. This is bachelor country, you know, and a lot of them come here regular. You'll be meeting some of them when you stay at that new hotel in town. It's a pretty nice place, lots of trophies on the wall and a few card games going on. It gets a bit lively sometimes. There's one fellow who likes to tap-dance on the tables. Usually he's had a bit too much of that Peace River Mist that a friend of his bottles.

So you're a bachelor too? Then you know what I mean when I talk about wanting to keep life simple. Are you getting along all right with that buggy of yours? You'll be glad the trail is so good now. Wagons go by all the time on the way to the Pouce Coupe prairie, all loaded up with household stuff. There's usually some poor lady bouncing around on the seat beside her husband while he hangs on to the reins. There are cars too, now and then. Of course you can't see who is in them 'til they stop because the windows are so black with mud. Everyone fixes up the bad spots on the road as they go along and that helps out the next fellow. You won't have much trouble.

You say you met a school inspector? Well I guess there aren't many of those around. Just like the nurse that the taxi man from Grande Prairie brought by last spring. She was the first one I'd seen in a long while. She was on her way to work at the Red Cross Hospital in Pouce. I kind of wished that I hadn't grown a beard when I saw her come through the door. I had just washed my shirt, too, so there I was with these suspenders over my underwear. I started to tell her how the doctor had stopped here last winter with a sick man in his sleigh, and how I hadn't charged him anything for the hot tea he wanted, and how I gave him a sack of turnips to take back, when she interrupted me and asked for another piece of pie. Well, I was flattered about that, and when I had it dished out I tripped somehow over that bear rug and spilled that darn blueberry pie all over her. She laughed about it and I helped her clean up as best as I could so she'd be presentable again before she left.

Since you're a bachelor too, you'll know how surprised I was that evening to find myself thinking about making life a little more complicated. I was sitting around playing solitaire and was saying to myself that maybe my life was a bit too simple and maybe I would like some company, and you know, the way the lantern light was flickering it looked like that old bear on the floor was winking at me. I kind of wondered if he had tripped me on purpose.

A few days later, I noticed that my thinking was still a bit jumbled, so I went out to work on the woodpile to settle myself down. I started chopping wood and was remembering how clumsy I'd been, spilling that pie, and how untidy I must have looked that day, with a beard and no shirt, when the axe slipped and cut right through my overall and into my leg. There was blood shooting all over the place and I could even see the bone all white and shiny in there. I hobbled into the house and was wrapping it up the best I could when my friend Buzz, who has the sawmill down the way, happened by with his team and a load of lumber. That was a lucky thing. I had been talking to him the day before about making this place a bit bigger and had asked him to bring me some boards. He unloaded the lumber and put me in his wagon and took me to the hospital. And who do you think was the first person I saw? That's right. There she was, all neat and dressed in white and making jokes about my pie.

You were hoping that you would meet a few girls along this route? Not much chance. Well, yes, I had to stay in the hospital for a week or so, so I had a chance to watch her quite a bit. She was busy, what with women coming in from miles away to have their babies, and people so sick with pneumonia and such. One poor family had two little boys die with that terrible polio disease. I watched how nice she was to all those people and how bright and pretty she was every morning, and I got to thinking she might be just the sort of person to have around all the time. I thought I might ask her to a dance sometime, before the snow flies, now that my leg's healed.

So you like to dance? And you are going to stop at the hospital to find out where to deliver the mail bag?

You know, the next ten-mile stretch on this road is very bad. I don't think that buggy of yours looks strong enough to make it through. I think I'll saddle up and ride along with you. It's no trouble at all. I can take you right to the post office. Getting that mail to Pouce is important and I'd hate to think of it lost in some mud hole. You look like the type of fellow who might need some help if you break down. I'm handy at fixing things. Don't mind a bit, helping you out. I've been wanting to go in anyway to ask that little nurse a question. I've been wondering how she likes the simple life, and could she enjoy the sound of coyotes and wolves howling in the night.

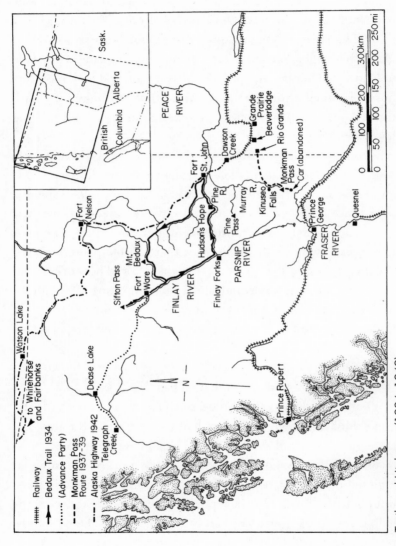

Trails and Highways (1934–1942)

CHRONICLE

Riverboats soon replaced the steamboat on the river and in 1931 the railway from Edmonton was extended to Dawson Creek. The Peace River Block, by that time, had been transferred from federal to provincial control. Thousands of homesteads were filed on and many settlers from the dried-out prairies took up land in the region called the Peace. The countryside began to change as small homes and rough roads were built. Land was cleared, and schools and churches became the beginnings of new towns. As the people came, so did the world-wide depression. Settlers had to be self-sufficient as there were no markets and there was no money. The river, though, remained an attraction for wealthy adventurers.

THE BEDAUX EXPEDITION [10]

1934

"I could run the universe,"
Said Mr. Charles Bedaux,
"For I have lots of money
And I live in a chateau.
My friends are mostly presidents
And chancellors and kings
And I have spent my life
Doing most amazing things.

"I've crossed the dry Sahara
And sailed the southern seas.
I've hunted game in Canada.
I live just as I please.
I like to seek adventures
That others frown upon,
And now I start a new one
Near the Peace at Fort St. John.

"For when I hunted game,
At Hudson's Hope to be specific,
I saw that people there could use
A route to the Pacific.
So I've returned to drive some cars
Where roads do not exist.
A challenge that's impossible
Is what I can't resist.

---

10 See note on page 155.

"I've brought along my special crew
Of forty-four or more.
The gamesman is from Scotland.
The mechanic is a bore.
The cameraman from Hollywood
Has skills you won't believe.
The dispatcher will send messages
For newsmen to receive.

"A geologist and one who maps
Are also to be paid.
My wife and my companion
Have insisted on a maid.
There's also a surveyor,
A commander and a cook,
And then of course, there is the one
Who'll help me write a book.

"I've brought a folding bathtub
And a case of caviar.
I've cutlery and crystal
And a specialty cigar.
The tents are all quite fire-proof,
I've cushions and I've rugs,
And I have special potions
To keep away the bugs.

"I've hired a hundred cowboys
To pack the gear each day.
The parties in advance have gone
To clearly mark the way.
The cars are half-track vehicles.
All five are nickel-plated.
The strength of Citroëns like these
Has been well demonstrated.

"The camera will be rolling
As I start my long parade.
I'll go twelve hundred miles
On a road that's not yet made
Through the acres of the wilderness
That stretch out north and west.
I'm a modern-day explorer
And I am the very best

"When we cross the Rocky Mountains
In my special motor cars,
I'll reach into the heavens
And touch the brightest stars,
For I could run the universe
If I had but half a chance.
My politics, so obvious,
Have no significance."

And so the expedition,
With twenty tons of goods,
Went north beyond the river
And travelled through the woods.
The ponies in the pack train
Carried things like ladies' shoes.
Some even struggled bravely
With crates of bubbly booze.

The vehicles were useless
In the muskeg and the rain.
They were lowered down ravines
And winched back up again.
They were rafted over rivers
And stuck in stump-filled roads.
Their abandonment was filmed
In dramatic episodes.

The travellers, on horseback,
Continued, while the guide
(From the mountains high in Switzerland)
Helped Bedaux decide
How to carry the essentials
And discard the other things.
The Bedaux expedition
No longer lived like kings.

But they rode across the mountains
And reached a river there
That led them to the Finlay
And the place known as Fort Ware,
Where Mr. Charles Bedaux
Said the riding days were done
As winter was approaching
And the wilderness had won.

He hired boats to travel
As canoes had done before
Down the swiftly flowing rivers
'Til he heard the canyon's roar.
He tarried for a day or two
To contemplate his fame,
Knowing now that maps would show
A mountain with his name.

Then some began to wonder
As the mood became subdued
Why the money had been spent
And what the failed attempt had proved.
But as he looked behind him
Bedaux was heard to say,
"I've walked among the Gods
On the mountains up that way."

PEGGY'S DIARY

1935

AUGUST 25, 1935

This train trip is terrible. Not too bad out of Vancouver and through the Rockies, but north of Edmonton there is nothing to see but bush. Sat up all night to save the cost of a berth. No sign of lights anywhere along the way.

AUGUST 30, 1935

The Chairman of the School Board met me at the station. The town didn't look like much, but nevertheless, I hated to see those few buildings vanish into the distance behind me. We drove out here on a dusty, bumpy road and I broke the heel off my shoe as I was coming in to have a look at the school. To think there were over two hundred applications for this job!

SEPTEMBER 3, 1935

Why did I ever come? The train trip was bad enough, but now I'm here, boarding with strangers, and scared to death about my first day of teaching tomorrow. Hope fate will be kind to me!

SEPTEMBER 4, 1935

The children behaved quite well, even though the bigger boys are taller than me. Some had walked over three miles to get to school.

Glad that my boarding house is just across the road. Mrs. Miles had tea ready for me when I got home.

SEPTEMBER 10, 1935

A lot of the children ride horses to school and I'm afraid of horses! Even had to set a mousetrap tonight. Tomorrow I may have to empty it! We played baseball at recess. I'm learning how to keep score.

SEPTEMBER 15, 1935

The farmer down the road helps with the janitor work and keeps the water barrel filled. He was curious about why I came. Didn't like to tell him that it was the pay. The rate is twice as high here as in Vancouver. He told me to call him Bill.

SEPTEMBER 25, 1935

Have never seen so many preserves. People must can everything that grows around here. They usually give me some when they have me over for dinner. I even tasted rose hip jam.

SEPTEMBER 30, 1935

Not much reading material in the school for the children. Glad I brought some story books to read aloud. One boy taught himself to read from the Eatons catalogue.

OCTOBER 10, 1935

Went into town and stayed over with some teachers there. Big dance on Saturday night. Met a young banker who told me outrageous stories about last summer's floods. Claimed that the railways were washed out and the roads were under water. Gave me an idea for the Christmas concert. I'll use a Noah's Ark theme.

OCTOBER 15, 1935

The Anglican missionary lady from Fort St. John brought out Sunday School books for the district. Made me think I was in darkest Africa, especially with the way the days are shortening. Have heard about some adventurous men that live around here. One grew up in Singapore and another cruised down the Yangtze River. Now they are farming. Hard to understand.

NOVEMBER 5, 1935

Glad to have Bill looking after the fires on these cold mornings. The children are so bundled up when they arrive for class I hardly know who is coming through the door. Was surprised to find that people even try to preserve winter around here! The dugouts are frozen, so Bill brings big blocks of ice to the school to melt for water. He cuts them from the river and keeps them in sawdust. Wedding dance at the school last Saturday. Lots of fun. The banker and others came out from town.

DECEMBER 10, 1935

Had dinner at Bill's—thought it would be all right, even though he lives alone. I've been to all the other houses. He showed me some old articles from *The Province* that he'd saved, all about the beautiful Peace River and the wonderful farm land. Said that reading them brought him up here. They were written a few years ago by a Mr. Johnson. Hope my fate is better than that poor man's. He vanished after interviewing Hitler in Germany.

DECEMBER 15, 1935

No time for diary writing. Busy with costumes for the concert. I'm sure these children never see their parents in daylight now, the days are so short. It's nice to be able to see the light in the house across the road when I leave from school. Can even see the light in Bill's house down the road. Never thought I'd be so interested in seeing lights!

JANUARY 10, 1936

Spent Christmas with Aunt Agnes in Edmonton. Had fun telling her all about the concert. Everyone in the district came and there were lots of laughs. Hard to get used to the city again. Not sure it was worth all the money it cost to go out.

JANUARY 20, 1936

Very cold. Mrs. Miles laughed when I told her the thermometer must be broken because it said fifty below. They say it will only last a few weeks. Kind of pretty walking over to the school on these frosty mornings.

JANUARY 30, 1936

Found out what a chinook wind does. The thermometer went from forty below to forty above in a couple of hours! Bill told me that the banker I met has been transferred. Wedding dance at the school on Saturday.

FEBRUARY 9, 1936

Still using blocks of ice from the river for water. I find I drink a lot because the heat from the school stove makes the air so dry. Lots of measles and other things going around. Heard about someone being flown to the hospital in the city the other day. The district nurse went with them. Hard to believe that there are airplanes in a primitive place like this. Planes come from Edmonton and Vancouver and go even farther north. Must be a lot better than teams of dogs or horses!

MARCH 19, 1936

No time for diary writing. School keeps me busy. Lots of wedding dances too. Mrs. Miles has taught me to quilt. Am going to learn to ride a horse when the mud dries up.

APRIL 23, 1936

The school inspector came by—seemed pleased with the progress the children have made. Wants to know what my plans are for next year. Who knows what fate holds in store? The dugouts are filling with the spring runoff. The snow seemed to go overnight. Wonder if the trees will ever have leaves on them again?

MAY 18, 1936

Summer came today with a bang! Don't know why there is no spring weather. Have just learned the local legend. Apparently if you drink the waters of the Peace you will return to live near its shores. Do you suppose that's why Bill brought all those blocks of ice? Can hardly sleep at night with all this daylight. Don't need any lights now!

JUNE 29, 1936

End of school! Had a picnic today, with a ball game. Bill was a great help. Leave for home tomorrow. Plan to do a lot of sewing this summer as I think my fate is sealed. The next wedding dance around here may be mine.

PATHFINDERS[11]

1936-1938

We are forgotten people
in the Peace,
ninety thousand of us,
isolated
in our rich empire
by muskeg and mountains
and government indifference.
Here we live
with twice Ontario's fields
and twice the prairie yields
and no route west.
Only the Peace
crosses the mountains,
or maybe a horse,
on the Pine Pass trail.
And so our grain and stock are shipped
eight hundred extra miles
through Edmonton
as we remain
forgotten.

---

11 See note on page 155.

There is an answer.
A pass is known
near waterfalls.
It has seen the footprints of hunters
and other men
who know the way.
Listen to Mr. Monkman.
He has been there.
He says the pass is low
and wide
and ready.
One hundred and thirty-two miles
is all that separates the end of our present road
and the rail that runs
to Prince George.
We will build the way ourselves
and cross the alpine meadows
with a car.

Come, you volunteers.
Come, blaze the trail to prosperity.
You will hear the roar of the Murray River
dropping over two hundred feet
at Kinuseo Falls.
The cascades beyond
lead to a lake
that rivals Louise
in beauty
reflecting the mountains we must cross.
Our road will be known
in all the land
and we will no longer be
forgotten.

CAMPED BY KINUSEO FALLS [12]

September 1939

The car rests near our goal
but the dream must die.
The roar of water cannot drown
the sounds
of war.

TOMSLAKE [13]

Summer 1939

Travellers have come,
five hundred and more.
They have resisted
marching boots
and seen the shadows of Munich
that show bitter times ahead.
Five thousand miles
on ship and train,
time to wonder
again and again,
are the others still alive?
Do wolves now wait for us in Canada?
So here they are,
with the mosquitoes,
in bare shacks.
They have been given
scythes and saws
and told to farm,
peasant-like,
in uncleared fields.
Eight hundred years their families lived
   in the Sudetenland
and now they are here,
travellers,
who must learn
to milk and plant
and find water in creeks that freeze.
This is their new Sudetenland,
so cold, so quiet,
so safe, so free.

---

13 See note on page 156.

THE CHANGING PEACE

CHRONICLE

World War II began in 1939 and its effects reached even the land of the Peace. The Japanese presence in the Aleutian Islands was seen as a threat of possible invasion, so the American and Canadian governments combined their interests to build a fifteen-hundred-mile highway from Dawson Creek in the Peace country to Fairbanks, Alaska. This road, built as a security measure, followed a route that connected the already established airports. Many miles of the route were parallel to the Bedaux trail. Completion of the highway meant that the Peace River was spanned by a bridge at Taylor, near Fort St. John, in August 1943, and the people of the Peace had access to the north. With the end of the war the Alaska Highway became the lifeline to communities beyond the railway.

MILE ZERO

1950

This town is really a collection of shacks, thought Katie, as she looked out the window in the grey light of early morning. She knew there were some attempts at fencing and gardens, but that was downtown. Up on the hill where she now lived with Rupert, the roads were usually muddy when they weren't frozen, and there were no sidewalks. The reason they lived on the hill, her brother had explained, was to enjoy the view. Rupert liked to look out of the same window and see the beginnings of the Alaska Highway down below as it stretched past the elevators and away from the town.

The winter sunrise began to creep over the ridge of hills to the east. Katie drank her tea and watched the huge, empty sky fill with colours. Those are garden colours, she thought, like my roses at home. She was glad the night was over. It was during the long hours of darkness that the pain in her hip bothered her the most. She would feel better as the day progressed.

The back door opened and Rupert came into the kitchen where Katie sat. He stamped the snow from his boots and dropped an armful of wood into the box by the stove. The cold air clung to him. Katie tightened her sweater around her shoulders.

"Do you need anything?" Rupert asked. "I'll be gone all day."

He worked hard, this brother of hers, thought Katie. It had

been summer when she arrived from England to live with him. He often came home late, even then, from his trips up the highway. He would arrive dusty and tired, his truck covered with mud. Now it was ice and snow that he battled. Trucking paid well, but it seemed to Katie that it was work for a younger man. She knew that stories of the highway had brought him to the area. He had been excited by reports of miles of new country opened up in just eight months of wartime construction. She was sure that Rupert thought of himself as a modern-day voyageur, with a highway, not a river, to explore.

Katie stood by her chair and reached for her cane as she answered. "I'll be fine," she said. "I'm going to paint. It keeps my mind off the cold. I worry about you when you go on these trips."

"You don't need to worry," said Rupert. "I know every turn in the road. When spring comes I'll take you along for a little adventure. There's a river you'll like, the Kiskatinaw, about twenty miles up. It has a nice curved bridge and high cutbanks, and a good spot to picnic."

"I crossed the ocean," said Katie, half laughing. "That's adventure enough for now."

Rupert smiled as he warmed his gloves at the stove. "I guess we can dream in different directions," he said. He gave a wave as he went out the door.

Katie watched him from the window. The truck, loaded with lumber, was parked in the yard. Rupert, in his long jacket and fur hat, was carrying a broom. He began to sweep the snow from the windows and windshield of the truck, his face almost hidden by the white puffs that marked his breathing. The truck, too, was half hidden in clouds of white exhaust that grew as the motor idled. Beyond the truck, out over the town, columns of white smoke reached straight up from the chimney of each of the many houses in the valley, creating a pattern against the brilliant blue of the sky. Blue and white, those are the colours of the morning now, she thought. She could see, near the ridge of hills to the south, the beginnings of the highway that led to Grande Prairie, and disappearing into the gradual rise of land to the west, the Alaska Highway, where Rupert would be going. She heard the crunching of the snow as the truck pulled away. She knew that it must be very cold.

Katie added wood to the fire before she cleared away the breakfast dishes and set up her painting supplies. She liked to paint scenes of England, of lovely stone or brick homes with gardens full of roses and greenery, or maybe of fog coming across the sand and winding itself around houses and cliffs. Sometimes she would add children, playing on the beach, but this would remind her too much of the days she had known before the war, when her son was young, and she would paint over the figures. She had tried a few times to paint a Canadian scene, with snow, as it was today, sparkling and drifted into waves, but this had never worked well for her. Perhaps she would feel differently if she had lived here when she was young, like the children she saw now, walking down the road outside on their way to school. There were several of them sliding on the icy surfaces as they balanced books and lunches, some walking backwards to be part of the group. They were as rosy and pervasive as the sunrise had been.

She had been surprised to find that there were other people who painted in this northern town. There was a talented group, women mostly, who met regularly. The town even had a library and a florist. The isolation, especially in winter, seemed to bring people together. They met to play bridge, to watch films, to put on plays, to discuss new highway links, or to plan new hospitals. These were things Katie had never experienced, and Rupert involved her in them all. She hadn't known that a community could be built from nothing, the way people wanted it to be. Just as there were no old buildings, there were no restricting traditions. Everything was new, even the radio station. If only the town had more trees.

Rupert knew it was cold as he drove down the hill. The truck's steering was stiff and the ride was as rough as one in an old horse-drawn farm wagon. The intersection where he turned onto the highway was sanded, so he had no difficulty slowing down. He pulled into the gas station a few blocks along to gas up. Another truck pulled in behind him as he parked. Rupert got down out of his cab and walked back to talk to the other driver. "Going to Fort Nelson, Jack?" he said to the tall man with a big grin who greeted him.

"That's right," was the reply. "And you?"

"Just to Fort St. John," Rupert answered. "I don't like to leave Katie alone at night in the winter."

"I told you she'd probably hate it here," said Jack. "You shouldn't have asked her to come."

"She decided herself," said Rupert. "Thought it would be better than being alone."

"Maybe so," said Jack. "Anyway, I won't be far behind you. Hope they've sanded the hills."

"Guess we'll know soon enough," was the reply.

Rupert paid for his gas and climbed back into the truck. Soon he was following the highway past the elevators and out of town, heading northwest. He wondered as he drove what Katie was doing. He hoped that she would paint today. She seemed to spend a lot of her time looking out of the window. He knew it was hard for her here in winter. She was frightened of walking outside when it was icy, and she did not know how to drive. Being on a few committees helped; she could take care of details on the phone. She often had visitors, too, other newcomers in town, and she liked to read with the radio for company. Maybe it had been wrong to let her come. He had lived with her in England fifteen years earlier before he came to Canada, and they had got along well in spite of their ten-year age difference. She had been a war widow then with a young son to raise, and he had enjoyed the boy. Then damned if the boy wasn't killed at Normandy. To lose a husband in one war and a son in another was pretty tough. Now she had arthritis to trouble her. At least it was in her hip and not her hands. She could still paint. Anyway, she was family. He had to have her here.

Rupert loosened his jacket and took off his gloves as the truck cab warmed up. He enjoyed getting out on the highway. Driving on a morning like this, when the air was so still, he felt like he owned this empty land. He could see for miles across the fields and the clumps of brush in the clear, cold air. Farther along, beyond the Kiskatinaw, he would be able to see the mountains, white and sharp, on the horizon. If he could paint like Katie, he would do a winter scene. He would show how every branch and twig was etched in hoar frost, white and feathery, against the sky. Even the barbs on the fencing wire were covered today. White and blue, the colours of winter, with black for fence posts and spruce. That's what needed to be shown.

The highway curved ahead, enclosed by banks of snow. The downward grade shone, even in the shadow of the hill. Rupert pushed on the brake pedal as the truck picked up speed. He was halfway down the hill that approached the bridge. He was going too fast to make the turn onto the wooden platform that continued in an arc to the far side of the river. The frail bridge railings would never stop a truck. He pumped the brakes. The rear of the truck began to swing from side to side, towards the high bank on his left one moment and then towards the ditch on his right. He felt the load of lumber shift and knew the truck was rolling over before he lost consciousness.

———————

Katie turned on the radio and started to clean her paintbrushes. She had done all the painting she would do today. She had soup to warm up for lunch and then she would read awhile. The radio program amused her. It was Hospital Bulletins. Each day at noon, the names and conditions of the thirty or so patients in the hospital were broadcast. The weights of all the new babies would be given and people up the highway would be advised if a child or an adult could go home. The announcer had just started to discuss an accident when she saw the Mountie coming to her door. She limped across the room to answer his knock.

"Rupert's been hurt," said the policeman. "I'll drive you to the hospital." Katie couldn't answer. She held the door frame and motioned the man inside. She had met him before. He curled with Rupert and had been by once for coffee after a game. He helped her find her boots and coat and held her arm as she went to his car. As they drove down the hill he explained that it had been Jack who had come upon Rupert's overturned truck.

Katie hardly heard what else he said as he left her on the first floor of the hospital. The Sister on duty had her sit in a small lounge and brought her a cup of tea. The Doctor, gruff and fatigued, arrived to talk to her. She felt his hand tighten on her shoulder as he explained that the fractures and frostbite would heal. She knew that he and Rupert had fished the rivers together, sharing campfires and rum.

Rupert was sleeping when she finally saw him. His leg was elevated on a pillow and encased in plaster. Wet plaster and ether—the room smelled of both. Katie felt nauseated. She was grateful when Mary from her painting group appeared and offered to drive her home.

The arch in the western sky was darkening as they reached the house. There was a fresh powdering of snow in the yard, marked by tires and boots. Mary said that she would be back the next day to drive Katie to the hospital.

Katie went into the house. As she turned on the light in the kitchen, she saw a loaf of warm bread on the table and a pan of stew on the stove. The fire was banked and the woodbox was full. By her chair in front of the window was a bouquet of small roses trimmed with ribbons and pieces of spruce. The shadows and scents greeted her, comforted her.

She took off her coat and boots and sat in her chair. She could hear a chinook wind starting to encircle the house. She knew what she would do tomorrow. She would do a picture for Rupert. She would get out her paints and start with blue and white and add the colours of a sunrise. She would show a highway and hills and maybe a river. She would paint this new world she had found, this cold, white world so full of warmth and colour, and of friendly people without pasts. And in the spring she would plant a tree.

CHRONICLE

*With peacetime came prosperity and development. The
population of the Peace country doubled with the discovery of gas
and oil. A highway through the Pine Pass was completed in 1952
and a railway from the west arrived in 1958. The Peace River
country finally had access to the province of British Columbia, and
the river was no longer essential for transportation. The mystique
of the river's wilderness, however, remained.*

THE RIVERBOAT MAN

1962

an interview at the Peace

You ask me why I do this? Why I jump in my boat and push away from the banks of the river whenever I can? Why I spend all this money on gas to run a boat just for fun? Well, I guess if you had made a trip or two with me you might understand.

I feel all crowded up sometimes in town. When I get out on the river and there is nobody upstream or downstream for miles, I feel as free as those eagles that glide around in the sky. The motor on the boat will purr like a kitten, when it's running right, and it makes just enough noise so I don't have to talk to whoever I'm with. I just keep quiet so I can enjoy the sound of the water against the boat. I might point out a moose or a bear on shore along the way, but that's about all.

There's always lots of time for talk when we make camp in the evening. We usually try to catch a few grayling for supper and cook them over the fire. That's another time when things seem pretty nice, when the fish are browning in the pan and the coffee is brewing. Sure there are a few mosquitoes and sometimes the weather is bad, but boats like mine are forty feet long and there is lots of room to carry tents and other gear to keep comfortable.

One of the best things about making these trips is getting to know the river. There's a few weeks during the spring runoff when you have to watch for snags of roots or branches but most of the time the river is clear and steady and you can trust it, like an old friend, as long as you give it lots of respect.

I often put the boat in right here, near this bridge on the Alaska Highway. Yes, that's the bridge that fell down a few years ago. One half just collapsed into the river. The towns around here were booming right then, with pipelines and refineries being built, and people needed to cross the river. They put planks down on the railway bridge, and when the trains weren't coming, they drove across there. In the winter, if they were brave enough, they went straight across the river on the ice.

I'm going to make a run from here, where the Pine joins the Peace, to just below the canyon. That's where the old Rocky Mountain Portage House used to be, before there was a Hudson's Hope. No, you can't see the canyon by boat. You have to drive in, to where the old coal mine was.

Yes, I've been up the Finlay. I've been up the Parsnip, too, to Arctic Lake. That's where Alexander Mackenzie went on his way to the Pacific. It was pretty exciting to know that what I was seeing was the same as what the explorers saw.

The best river trip has always been the one on the Peace, between the top of the canyon and Finlay Forks. The rapids could be a problem if you weren't careful, even with these twenty-five horsepower motors. A fellow drowned up there not long ago. His boat lost power in the Ne Parle Pas and capsized. That water is too cold for anyone to survive in for very long.

There are some sights on the river up there that I'll never forget. The one I like the best is on the other side of the pass. If you look to the east, you'll see Mt. Selwyn, with its reflection in the river, the trees green and gold on the slopes and the peaks covered with snow. If you look to the west you'll see the Wolverine Mountains, purple, on the horizon, with the water in the Finlay Rapids boiling white in front of them. There'll usually be birds and beavers around and some old moose having a drink from the river. There aren't many sights much prettier than that.

That valley above the canyon has always seemed like another world to me. There were never any roads into the wilderness, just rivers. A hundred years ago, when the gold rush was on, the miners said it was a valley of death. Now there's another kind of rush on and it's going to mean the death of the valley. There are forestry crews and engineers along the river, and there is so much machinery noise in the canyon you can hardly hear the water. There's going to be a dam built across the top of the canyon and it's like the end of my world. The only dams around here up 'til now have been the ones made by beavers. I wonder what Alexander Mackenzie would have to say. He predicted that some day the canyon would be conquered.

I've had my last trip above the canyon. That part of the river is older than the Rocky Mountains and it's soon going to be gone. The river is going to be a big lake, which can be a pretty sight, but it can't compare to a river. A river is alive. I guess that's the real reason I like having a riverboat. Being on the river makes me feel alive.

When we were coming home on that last trip, we stopped for the night near Bernard Creek. We had a good fire going and it was peaceful, like it should be, with the sounds from the creek and the river. There was some good-natured talk going on in the dark around the fire when the northern lights started dancing across the sky in a way that I'd never seen. They were as jagged and bright as the flames of the fire, and they sounded like a fire, too. It was as though we were being told to remember the power of the Peace. That's the real reason I agreed to talk to you. Everyone should respect the power of this river and I hope you will tell them.

A DREAMER SPEAKS

1964

The spirit of the swan
will watch
as the river
covers the hills.
Our hunters will dream
new trails
so we can know the safety of the peaks
forever.

CHRONICLE

After thousands of years, change came to the river.

In the cold of winter the upper end of the canyon was crossed by a cable, then straddled by a bridge. Tunnel drillers crossed to the far side and blasted, like the forces of ancient times, one million tons of rock. Three tunnels were built, each one the width of a four-lane highway. The course of the river that had once been changed by glaciers was diverted through the tunnels, and three thousand feet of the river bed were bare.

Four miles away, where the river so long ago had been blocked by the glacier, bulldozers and trucks as large as dinosaurs carried one-hundred-ton loads of gravel and placed them on a conveyor belt to be moved to the bare river bed and fashioned into a dam. The glacial deposits that had changed the course of the river in ancient times were once again in the river's path.

The canyon echoed to the sounds of drills and trucks as the dam grew. A powerhouse was built and transmission lines stretched across the mountains.

The tunnels were closed and the water behind the dam became a huge lake. It filled the valley of the upper Peace and extended into the trench that held the Finlay and Parsnip rivers.

The rapids were gone and the homes and the history were submerged.

Water flowed through the dam. All the energy that once cut through a mountain range poured onto turbines, and the power of the river spread across the land.

A PIONEER VOICE

1975

Gentle, gentle are the hills
That close around this land,
Holding out that other world,
Where few can understand
Why many came and never left
The land we call the Peace,
Where ground is often frozen
And rivers choke with ice.

But rivers in the springtime
Find freedom in the sun,
And we, who settled northward,
Found, when day was done,
That gentle hills for touching
Made our lives seem real,
As valleys glowed in sunlight
With each season's new appeal.

IMAGES

1978

The morning light filtered through the stained glass windows of the church as Ed Martin sat down. He was glad to feel the warmth from the sun on his shoulders. He had walked the several blocks from his house and was chilled. He listened to the music from the organ as people settled into the pews ahead. He saw Clara's son and daughter arrive with their families. Some of the others would be nieces and nephews, or maybe neighbours. They all carried a memorial card, like the one that had been given to Ed at the door. It was an agenda, really, for the service that was about to begin. He moved along the pew to make room for a latecomer as the minister began to speak.

"This is a celebration of life," said the man in the pulpit. "We are here to remember the life of Mrs. Clara Benson. She didn't mind being called Clara, but the name Mrs. Benson seemed to suit her best, perhaps because she was proud to have been a teacher many years ago. She remained a keen student throughout her long life. I'm sure that most of you know what a great interest she had in history, especially the history of this Peace River region. She and her late husband came here with their young family before the railway arrived, moving here from the Saskatchewan prairies."

Ed half-listened to the words as they were spoken. How could this person know anything at all about Clara? The man was new in town. He'd only been around a few months. Ed looked at the small bulletin in his hand that listed the facts of her life and death. He began to fold the paper. He had certainly called her Clara. He was her only contemporary here, as far as he could see. The others were either dead or senile or too incapacitated by age to come. That was the trouble with living so long; you outlived those you could relate to.

There was singing and organ music. Ed wondered if Clara had chosen the hymns. She would have had lots of time to give a few orders about her funeral during the weeks she was in hospital. Ed had visited her there a few times. They had laughed as they talked, remembering things that had happened so long ago. When they talked of sleigh rides, of tumbling off in the snow and running to catch up, Clara had remembered the winter landscapes full of moonlight. When they recalled skating on the frozen slough before the snow came, Clara reminded him how the ice would echo as they glided along, and how it was sometimes so clear they could see grasses trapped and bent under the surface. There were the dances to talk about too. Clara had been very funny imitating the sound of heavy feet stomping to the rhythm of a loud piano. She had laughed as well about their sing-songs, before the radio came, when the only songs they knew were hymns and spirituals and maybe *Little Brown Jug*. No wonder his wife Mary had enjoyed her so much. Clara was someone who had absorbed all the bright images she had found in her life. She had even written poems about the wild flowers she enjoyed, like fireweed and Indian paintbrush. She had shown him her last poem. It was about the golden fields of ripening canola that were now part of the countryside in summer. As usual, she had tied it in with some history and some fun. He remembered only a few lines.

Mr. Toy, do you see this gold that's been found?
It ripples across the farmers' tilled ground.

It glimmers from hillsides in summer and fall
And gold you can grow is the best gold of all.

He had enjoyed remembering the good times with her. The four of them had needed the good times, back then, to blot out the bad. There was the isolation, the cold, the lack of money, the times when the children were sick and there was no doctor to call, and the years when the crops failed because of late springs or early frosts, and, of course, the sight of their sons leaving for war. There had been lots of bad times, but they had survived. They had given this part of the country its future.

Ed looked again at the memorial paper in his hand. He folded it lengthwise and gave it pleats and a point. It would fly now, he thought, if he sent it into the air. It could probably go the full length of the church and land on the casket. Clara would have been amused by him thinking like this. She would have understood, too, how hard it had been for him to come today. He was the last of them. His own Mary had gone three years before, and Tom, Clara's husband, a few years before that. What a trip it had been when they had all driven over that muddy road beyond the end of steel. They had met when they were coming north, both families looking for a promised land.

Ed stood for the benediction. He held the folded paper by its base and raised it shoulder high. What the hell, he thought. Here's to you, Clara. He gave the dart a quick thrust and it was on its way, over the heads of a few people and part way down the aisle. The young man standing beside him turned. What did I do that for, thought Ed. This boy will think I'm senile. The service was over and the rows ahead were emptying.

"You're Mr. Martin, aren't you?" The question came as Ed started to leave the pew.

"That's right," said Ed. The boy was older than he'd thought. He was a young man. He was about the same age his son had been when the bomber had gone down over Germany.

"I'm Dan Porter. I've been renting Mrs. Benson's cabin at the lake. I was at her house in town the night she fell."

"Damn rugs," said Ed. "That's how she broke her hip. She tripped on that damn rug at the door."

"I know," said Dan, as they walked to the back of the church. "Do you want a ride somewhere?"

"Maybe, " said Ed.

Clara's family was standing in the vestibule. Ed greeted them with affection and asked how long they would be in town. They wanted to know about his daughters and where they were living.

Ed buttoned his jacket as he stood on the church steps. The wind was cold in spite of the sun. He could hear the rustle of dried poplar leaves blowing across the bare sidewalk and the brittle, brown lawn. He was glad that he was without a car and couldn't drive to the gravesite. He turned to Dan, who was standing beside him. "Are you going to the lake?" he asked.

"You want to go to Moberly?"

"I want to get out of town. I'll take the bus back."

"Come on then," said Dan.

Ed followed Dan to the road and got into the younger man's pickup. "I appreciate this," he said, as Dan started the engine. They drove in silence for a few blocks. Ed looked straight ahead. He supposed he should try to talk to this stranger.

"I'm coming in tomorrow," Dan said. "I can bring you back. You can bunk at the cabin tonight if you want."

"I'd like that," was the reply. "I used to be there a lot." Dan opened a package as they reached the edge of town and handed Ed a sandwich.

"Guess you knew her a long time?" he asked. "Mrs. Benson, I mean."

"Most of a lifetime," said Ed. "We came here together, her husband and I."

They were travelling west of town on the Hart Highway. Ed looked out of the window at the fields of brown stubble, ready for winter. The ridge of foothills to the south was topped with snow. "The hunting should be good now," he said.

"It must have been great, hunting whenever you wanted, like you pioneers did. Mrs. Benson used to tell me about it."

"It's better now. You don't know what the gumbo was like."

"But it's not the same. It's lonely somehow."

Ed glanced at his companion. "Keep busy," he said. "You won't be lonely."

"I used to visit Mrs. Benson when I went in to pay the rent. I'll miss her." Ed didn't answer.

Soon the broad valley of the Pine River was before them. The Murray River could be seen as well, as it joined the Pine on its way to the Peace. "I had a riverboat trip up the Murray last summer," said Dan. "Went to Kinuseo Falls and camped there. It was pretty nice." He was driving down the long approach to the river as he spoke.

"Well then, you've seen something I've only heard about," answered Ed. "Guess that's a kind of pioneering."

"There should be a good road in there, to where the falls are."

"Then you'll have to do something about it," was Ed's reply. He noticed that the bridge over the Pine had been widened since his last trip out this way. Dan geared the truck down to make the climb up the winding hill that would take them back out of the valley. "Did you ever try fishing up the Pine?" asked Ed.

"No, but I've skied in the Pass. It's good powder snow."

"You have to fish before all the snow is gone. You walk in to Big Boulder Creek and strain the gravel in the creek for hellgrammites. That's the only bait to use. You'll get a bucketful of fish."

They drove on in silence until the next valley spread out ahead. "That used to be called Little Prairie," commented Ed, pointing to the community below. "They keep changing names around here nowadays. Can you imagine? They even changed a good name like Hungry Moose Creek. Just changed the sign without asking anybody."

Dan drove down the hill and turned north at the town. Ed knew the road. It led on past Moberly Lake to the town of Hudson's Hope on the Peace River. The bare poplars along the way were soon replaced by jackpine and spruce. "Have you seen the dam?" asked Dan.

Ed nodded. "That was some sight when it was being built. They had a tea room up on top and you could look down into the canyon and see the river going through the tunnels."

"That's where I'm working," said Dan. "I'm at the second dam, the one that's being built at the other end of the canyon. They'll be able to use all the water a second time, for more power."

"At least it means some pavement on these roads. I hauled coal out from Hudson's Hope a few times after the war. That canyon was a rare sight. The road to Fort St. John was pretty awful, though. Switchbacks all the way and fenders plugged with mud."

"The canyon will be filled with water when the dam's done."

"Well I guess we need the power," Ed replied. "I would have liked a job like yours when I was young. Imagine helping to take control of all that wild water."

The twin mountain peaks at the western end of the lake came into view and showed more fresh snow. Dan turned the truck onto the gravel road that accessed the south shore. "We used to walk in here," Ed observed.

"There's a tree down beside the cabin. I was going to cut it up today, if there's time." Dan wheeled off the road as he spoke and followed the trail that led to the cabin. He parked the truck in a clearing behind the small log building.

Ed was aware of the bush as he stepped out of the pickup. He could smell the leaves on the damp ground and could see the tangled peavine and the jumble of deadfall among the trees. The lake was ahead, beyond the cabin. "I'd better check the stove," said Dan.

Ed stayed outside, smelling the wood smoke from the chimney. He walked past the cabin and down the rough beach towards the water. The old firepit that he had helped Tom build was still there, and he noticed that the stream of spring water still drained into the lake. The fallen tree now filled the beach beside the stream, but something else was different as well. The shoreline shone in the sunlight. Splashing water had frozen into elaborate crystals on the rocks. The brilliant shapes were like miniature glass castles edging the lake. There was music, too. The sound was like a thousand chirping birds, or a thousand small bells, ringing. Sheets of ice, paper thin, chimed as they moved like waves on the surface of the lake. The sound was like that of tapped crystal.

These are sights and sounds of celebration, thought Ed. Here is music good enough to mark a life like Clara's, or any of our lives. Even in this late season I've found something new in this land, something unexpected, an image to remember. And he knew that what he had found would be like everything else in his life. It wouldn't last.

Dan came out of a shed by the cabin with two chain saws and an axe. He had changed his clothes and carried coveralls and a heavy plaid jacket for Ed. They both watched as the fragile ice beyond the glittering rocks began to shatter.

"I guess I'd better move back to the camp at Hudson's Hope soon," said Dan. "Looks like winter is coming." He went over to the fallen tree. It was a huge poplar. The trunk reached from the cabin to the edge of the lake. Ed joined him.

"I should still be able to handle one of these," he said, picking up a chain saw.

"I figured you could," said Dan with a grin.

Ed pointed towards the lake. A wedge-shaped ripple marked a beaver swimming by. The head disappeared as the slap of the tail on the water echoed into the woods.

"He thinks he could do a better job than us," said Ed with a laugh.

"River of Beavers," said Dan. "That's what the Peace was called. At least, that's what Mrs. Benson told me."

"She'd be right," said Ed. "Clara liked to talk about the beaver. She'd never let Tom trap the darn things. She wrote a poem about them once. Gave it as a recitation."

There was little more talk. Together they trimmed the branches and piled them near the bush. They bucked up the trunk and Dan rolled the blocks of wood to the side of the cabin. They worked easily together, each knowing what the other would do next.

The day was over when the job was done. Ed set up two chairs beside the firepit and built a fire. The flames flashed gently at first, nibbling at twigs and leaves. When the spruce logs began to burn, the sparks scattered, like new stars, into the increasing darkness. Dan brought a small pail from the cabin and filled it with cold water from the spring. He hung the pail on a rod over the flames and added coffee when the water boiled. He opened a package of wieners, ready for roasting. As they waited, the moon rose over the hills on the opposite shore and the reflected light shone across the lake. They could hear the waves on the beach and feel the heat from the fire. Soon the coffee, in mugs, was warming their hands, and the fatigue and loneliness had vanished.

CLARA'S RECITATION

The history of all this land
Is to the beaver bound.
A strange unlikely tale it is
For where else can be found
A country built because of fur,
The shiny beaver pelt,
That cured and cared for properly
Becomes a furry felt.

When Jacques Cartier went sailing west
In fifteen thirty-four
He hoped to find some treasure
On a distant Asian shore.
Instead he found a fishing ground
And took home in his hold,
Along with cod, some beaver furs,
In place of silks and gold.

But treasure sure is what he had
Although he did not know
For beaver furs were just the things
To make into chapeaux.
A fashion then was started
That stayed for centuries
Of beaver hats for gentlemen
To give them more prestige.

The army and the navy men
And all the clerics too
Were made to want a beaver hat.
What else was there to do
But send out from the shores of France
A man they called Champlain?
He was to live in that new land
And more fine furs obtain.

Champlain saw how the Indians
Travelled throughout the land
On thoroughfares of rivers
In canoes they made by hand.
Soon some brave and hardy men,
The coureurs de bois,
Were splashing down the river routes
Beyond the Ottawa.

The English thought they should compete.
They sailed into the bay
Where poor old Henry Hudson
Was put adrift one day.
They settled into fortresses
And let the paddlers bring
From all of Rupert's Land, the furs
From beaver slaughtering.

The French surrendered Canada
In seventeen sixty-three
And Scotsmen started trading
With a private company.
They followed rivers north and west
To reach the ocean shores
And bagpipe music could be heard
With singing voyageurs.

The trappers caught the beavers
The traders bought the furs
The plundering continued
For years and years and years
'Til all the lands were charted
And the beaver almost gone
Then fashion's whims were altered
And a beaver hat was wrong.

So the shiny little beavers
Were left to multiply
Their image on the nickel
Was meant to pacify.
But in your history lessons
Remember if you can
How the beaver led men northward
To where the river ran.

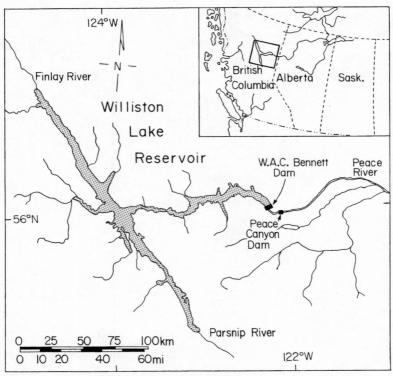

The Upper Regions of the Peace River (1980)

CHRONICLE [14]

The song of the river is finished for now. The canyon that defeated Mackenzie's voyageurs and almost killed Mr. Simpson's brave crew is conquered and there is a deep narrow lake behind the second dam. Men who worked there saw skeletons of reptiles, footprints of dinosaurs, and tusks of mastodons. Sometimes, when there was a moment of quiet, they wondered if they heard the sound of axes chipping an upward trail to the rhythm of a song.

The river has changed, but the waters of the ancient Peace still flow with majesty through the land that bears its name. If you travel on the river when the colours of fall are blazing on the slopes and the mountains on the horizon are a dazzling white, the river valley may fill with mist. If you listen, you will hear whispers from the past, nearby.

14 See note on page 156.

EPILOGUE

When you take a canoe on the river
Hear what your paddles can tell
Of the people who came to the river
To be touched by the river's spell.

If you walk in the mist near the river
You can to the river belong
For the river has been there forever
And the mist holds the river's long song.

NOTES

1. The First Nations people who are now called the Beaver have lived in the Peace country for thousands of years. There is evidence that a hunting society existed in the region for at least ten thousand and perhaps for as long as forty thousand years. Ancestors of the present groups probably hunted along the fringes of receding glaciers during the last ice age. The Beaver were members of the Athapaskan language group, whose culture became widespread in North America.

   Before 1750, three Athapaskan groups lived in the Peace region. The Beaver, who called themselves Dunne-za (the real people), hunted below the junction of the Peace and Smokey rivers to Lake Claire and Lake Athabasca. They may have extended as well along the valleys of the Athabasca and Clearwater rivers to the Methye Portage. The early fur traders did not understand the meaning of the term *Dene*. *Tsades*, or Beaver, was the name used by the First Nations people for the river that is now called the Peace. It was the Europeans who applied this name to the people.

   A second group, the Sekani, or dwellers among the rocks, lived on the Upper Peace and came as far east as the Peace-Smokey confluence. The third group, the Dunne-thah, known now as the Slavey, lived around Lake Athabasca.

   The fur trade affected these groups before Europeans arrived in the region. The Cree, who had acquired guns, pushed the Beaver farther west. The Sekani retreated west of the mountains and the Slavey moved farther north.

   In 1781, smallpox decimated the Cree. The Beaver acquired guns in 1782 and defeated the Cree that year. A treaty of peace was agreed upon, with the Beaver staying above the Peace-Smokey confluence and the Cree hunting east of the Peace. The name Unchaga, or Peace, became the name of the river.

   Nomadic because of their hunting culture, the Beaver travelled in small groups of two or three families. They had gathering places, or camps, rather than villages. A major camp was at the present location of Dunvegan, with lesser ones at Saskatoon Lake and Pouce Coupe. They were usually led by a respected hunter called a Dreamer. The dreams of these prophets were used to locate game.

2. Alexander Mackenzie, on his route to the Pacific, travelled to the headwaters of the Parsnip River, where a chain of three small lakes separates the Arctic and Pacific drainages. The lakes are appropriately named Arctic Lake, Portage Lake, and Pacific Lake. Later travellers followed the Pack River to Macleod Lake.

3. George Dawson travelled over two thousand miles by pack train, canoe, and wagon in 1879 as a member of the Geological Survey of Canada. He was the first Caucasian man to visit the present location of Dawson Creek.

4. Roman Catholic and Anglican missionaries began travelling the Peace as early as 1855. Anglican missions were established near Fort Vermilion, Peace River Crossing, and Fort Dunvegan.

5. A band of Ojibwa-speaking Salteaux, who had been on the move since the Riel Rebellion, arrived and settled at Moberly Lake in 1908. They had been seeking a location seen by their prophets in a dream, a long lake running east and west with twin peaks at the western end.

   Metis, some Cree and French, some Iroquois and French, also fled from the Riel Rebellion. They moved from Manitoba to Alberta in the late 1800s. Some came to the Peace area after 1900 and established a community at Kelly Lake.

6. The members of the Bull Outfit became the core of the future settlement of Beaverlodge, Alberta.

7. Material promoting the Peace was published by A.M. Bezanson and others. Newspapers in Edmonton and Vancouver contained advertisements that described the area in glowing terms.

8. Lucille and Jack Adams, who lived for a year near Finlay Forks in 1913, returned to the Peace after World War I and built a beautiful log home near Gold Bar, which they called *All's Well.*

9. The cost of freighting grain to Spirit River was estimated to be thirty cents a bushel. The revenue from one load out of every five would cover this cost. The route was abandoned in 1928 when the railway was extended to Hythe and the B.C. farmer could truck his grain to that point for twenty cents a bushel.

10. The Bedaux expedition might have succeeded if a report from the advance party had reached Fort Ware. A wire was sent from Telegraph Creek to say that a trail had been located and blazed, but the message was not received. Charles Bedaux was accused of treason by the American government in 1944 because of his suspected Nazi sympathies. He committed suicide before he could be brought to trial.

11. The Monkman Pass Highway Association was organized by Mr. Alex Monkman in 1936 in an attempt to provide Peace settlers with a shorter route to a coastal port. In the late fall of 1938 a pathfinder car was taken through the pass. It was abandoned on November 6 because of mechanical breakdowns and poor weather.

    In late August 1939, three women from Grande Prairie travelled over the route, going through the pass to Prince George. They were taken by truck as far as Kinuseo Falls, then were guided on horseback through the pass to the location of the pathfinder car. They were transported on by boat, down the Herrick and MacGregor rivers, and went on to Prince George by train. The newspaper report of their success was overshadowed by the news that war had been declared.

An unsuccessful attempt to cross the Monkman Pass from the west was organized in 1976 by Wayne Monkman, a grandson of Alex Monkman.

The pathfinder car was recovered in 1977, repaired, and placed in the Grande Prairie museum.

12. Kinuseo Falls on the Murray River is fifty feet higher than Niagara Falls. The water tumbles between solid rock walls that are three hundred and fifty feet apart. Monkman Park has since been established to prevent commercial development in the region.

13. Within the first year of their arrival at Tomslake, the Sudeten settlers, including 152 families, and thirty-seven single men, built a community hall, which became a centre for choir and theatre groups. Within four years, 107 individual farms were created. Other families moved on to employment in other areas of Canada. Forty-six of the young men in the group served in the armed forces during ww II. The first public library in the Peace River Block was opened at Tomslake in 1943 and other arts were developed and supported. Soccer was introduced to the area by the athletes among the group, and later skiing was promoted by those who missed the sport. The settlers were never indifferent to community responsibilities, and many became involved with local boards and governments. To mark the Canadian Centennial in 1967, the people of Tomslake built a stopping place for travellers, named Sudeten Park, on the highway near their community, in gratitude to their new homeland.

14. The W.A.C. Bennett Dam at the head of the Peace River Canyon was constructed between 1962 and 1967. The Peace Canyon Dam, 14 miles (23 kilometres) below, at the canyon's outlet, was built between 1975 and 1980. The two dams provide one third of British Columbia's power supply.

BIBLIOGRAPHY

Amstatter, A. *Tomslake*. Saanichton: Hancock House Publishers Ltd., 1978.

Angier, B. *Wilderness Neighbors*. New York: Stein and Day, 1978.

B.C. Hydro pamphlet. *The Peace: its past, its people, and its power*. n.d.

B.C. Hydro pamphlet. *Peace River Power*. n.d.

Berton, P. *The National Dream*. (Vol. 1).Toronto/Montreal: McClelland and Stewart, 1970.

Berwyn Centennial Association. *Brick's Hill, Berwyn and Beyond*. n.d.

Bonanza: Fellow Pioneers Historical Society. *Homesteaders' Heritage*. 1982.

Bowes, G.E. *Peace River Chronicles*. Vancouver: Prescott Publishing, 1963.

Brody, H. *Maps and Dreams*. Vancouver/Toronto: Douglas and McIntyre, 1981.

Calverly, D. *History is Where You Stand*. 1999. <http://www.calverly.dawson-creek.bc.ca>

Coutts, M.E. *Dawson Creek and District*. Dawson Creek Historical Society, 1958.

Coull, C. *A Traveller's Guide to Aboriginal B.C.* Vancouver/Toronto: Whitecap Books, 1996.

Debolt & District Pioneer Museum Society. *Edson to Grande Prairie Trail*, 1982.

Harper, M.L. *Faith in a Fertile Land*, n.d..

Kyllo, M.A. *Geographic Place Names Around Hudson's Hope*. Malakwa: Kyllo, 1992.

Leonard, D.W. & V.L. Lemieux. *The Lure of the Peace River Country*. Edmonton: Detselig Enterprises, 1992.

Lunn, J. & C. Moore. *The Story of Canada*. Toronto: Lester Publishing & Key Porter Books, 1992.

Macdonald, D. *Peace River Past*. Toronto: Venture Press, 1981.

MacGregor, J.G. *Homesteader's Trails to the Peace River Country*. Grande Prairie: Grande Prairie Pioneer Museum Society.

MacGregor, J.G. *History of Alberta*. Edmonton: Hurtig Publishers, 1972.

Myles, E. L. *The Emperor of the Peace River*. Saskatoon: Western Producer Prairie Books, 1978.

Newman, P.C. *Caesars of the Wilderness*. New York: Viking, 1987.

Marsh, J.H., ed. *The Canadian Encyclopedia*. Vols. 1, 2, and 3. Edmonton: Hurtig Publishers, 1985.

Pollen, E.K. & S. Smith-Matheson. *This Was Our Valley*. Calgary: Detselig Enterprises, 1989.

Ramsey, B. & D. Murray. *The Big Dam Country*. Vancouver: In Focus Publications, 1969.

Robinson, M. & D. Hocking. *The Monkman Pass and Trail*. Calgary: Petro-Canada Coal Division, 1982.

Ross, E. *Beyond the River and the Bay*. Toronto: University of Toronto Press, 1970.

Stacey, E.C. *Peace Country Heritage*. Saskatoon: Western Producer Book Service, 1974.

Stacey, E.C. *Beaverlodge to the Rockies*. Beaverlodge: Beaverlodge and District Historical Association, 1974.

Stanford, Q. H. *Canadian Oxford World Atlas*. Toronto: Oxford University Press, 1998.

Tanner, O. *The Old West*. Volume 1 –The Canadians. New York: Time-Life Books, 1977.

Truax, M. & B. Sheehan. *People of the Pass*. Grande Prairie: Menzies Printers, n.d.

Van Kleek, E. *Our Trail North*. Edmonton: Co-op Press Limited, 1980.

York, L., ed. *Lure of the South Peace*. Fort St. John/Dawson Creek: South Peace Historical Book Committee, 1981.

INDEX